So Now You Are A Goalkeeper

So Now You Are A Goalkeeper

Joseph A. Machnik
Frans Hoek

Phoenix Press, 15 James St., New Haven, CT 06513

About The Authors

Joe Machnik was born in New York City, January 13, 1943. He played high school soccer for Brooklyn Technical H.S. and collegiate ball for Long Island University, where he was named an All-American in 1962. Machnik has earned a Bachelor of Science and Masters of Science from L.I.U. and a Ph.D. from the University of Utah.

Joe Machnik holds the NCAA record for being the youngest head coach ever to coach in the National Championship game, a record achieved when L.I.U. appeared against San Francisco in the 1966 final. In thirteen years, Machnik's college teams appeared in eight post season tournaments and five national championship *"final fours."*

Machnik was a member of the 1965 National Challenge Cup Champions, New York Ukrainians and also played in the American Soccer League. He has long been noted for his expertise in coaching goalkeepers and has appeared in countless numbers of clinics and convention programs.

Machnik's No. 1 Goalkeeper's Camp was the first specifically goalkeeper camp to be organized on a national basis and the camp has produced top caliber goalkeepers at every level of play.

Machnik holds an "A" Coaching License from the United States Soccer Federation and has been a USSF Staff Coach. He coached in the first National Sports Festival and coached professionally with the New York Arrows of the Major Indoor Soccer League (MISL). He also was the MISL's Director of Operations and Referee-in-Chief, officiating the league's first game, first All-Star Game and first game at Madison Square Garden, and has served as Commissioner of the American Indoor Soccer Association.

In 1989 Machnik was named Assistant Coach—Goalkeeper Coach for the U.S. World Cup Team, which qualified for its first appearance in the World Cup Finals in forty years … its goalkeepers registering five shutouts in the eight game qualifying process.

"So Now You Are A Goalkeeper" is the sequel to the very popular "So You Want To Be A Goalkeeper," and will serve as the official text book of the advanced session of the No. 1 Goalkeeper's Camp.

Frans Hoek had been playing for the amateur club "Always Forward" in Hoorn until 1973 when he was called up to Volendam. Since then, he has been Volendam's goalkeeper almost uninterruptedly with two years play in the *"honors division"* and six years play in Holland's first division.

In addition, Frans Hoek has been selected to play on several representative teams; namely: twice for the Dutch National Youth Team (16-17 years of age); twenty times for UEFA Youth Select; eight times for Young Orange, Holland's *"B"* National Team and twice for the Dutch National Military Team.

Hoek's work on "So Now You Are A Goalkeeper" was done as part of his studies at CIOS- University. Frans Hoek has been a staff member at the No. 1 Goalkeeper's Camp and conducts similar goalkeeper clinics and camps throughout Europe.

His book "Everything About Goalkeeping" has been a best seller in Holland and throughout Europe. He is currently coach of goalkeepers for Ajax of Amsterdam, one of the worlds most famous soccer teams.

Foreward

It has often been said that soccer's goalkeeper has been a *"forgotten player."* Perhaps this was true during the 70's and first half of the 80's, but not so today. The proliferation of fundamental goalkeeping information has educated young goalkeepers and their coaches to a basic understanding and appreciation of the demands placed upon the goalkeeper and the contribution to team success that a goalkeeper at the top of his or her game may present.

Fifteen years of clinics, conventions, coaching schools, and the No. 1 Goalkeeper's program has eliminated much of the mystery which surrounds the goalkeeper. Twenty-five thousand copies of "So You Want To Be A Goalkeeper" have enabled a generation of goalkeepers to survive in the goal. But we have reached that point in time and the development of the game where survival is not enough.

The goalkeepers want more, coaches expect more and fans understand the difference.

It is now time for these goalkeepers and coaches, as well as, a developing cadre of supporters and detractors to leave the fundamental approach based largely on technique and concentrate on the production of goalkeepers who are tactically sound and can play according to the demands of today's game at every level.

It is time to discuss goalkeeping with the focal point being the significance in winning rather than the subject around which to blame defeat.

The coaching of goalkeepers is hardly just the presentation of drills and exercises, the use of a forty second timer and a loud voice. It is match analysis, mental training, the development of relationships on and off the field and honest effort at solving problems by presenting and working out appropriate solutions.

To do this requires a willingness to participate in endless hours of practice for one save for one game, and the ability for the goalkeeper and coach to mutually understand the process. SO NOW YOU ARE A GOALKEEPER provides the highest level of written goalkeeping instruction yet presented in the United States. I believe that it has what it takes to become the new bible for American goalkeepers and I wish you the very best in achieving its potential.

Joseph A. Machnik, President
No. 1 Goalkeeper's Camp

For some time now, I have looked for a vehicle to share the goalkeeping expertise which I have developed in Holland with American goalkeepers, especially the youth about which we hear so much even overseas.

After meeting and working with Joe Machnik at the No. 1 Goalkeeper's Camp, and being fully witness to his program and method of instruction, I am convinced that he is among the finest goalkeeper instructors in the world, and in many countries has no parallel.

I am pleased to share my life-time of study with Americans through Joe Machnik and will continue to endeavor to develop modern training ideas as the game continues to change for the goalkeeper.

Frans Hoek, Goalkeeper
Ajax of Amsterdam

Acknowledgements

The publication of a text as detailed and scientific as SO NOW YOU ARE A GOALKEEPER, especially in light of the responsibility of knowing its impact on the soccer community and the study of goalkeeping in particular is not a task which is easily performed without the participation of a great many professionals and loyal family supporters and friends.

The work of Frans Hoek in Holland, along with journalist Jaap de Groot and photographer, Hans Van Tilburg must be acknowledged as the single most important contribution to the study of goalkeeping in modern times. Also thanks to Dr. J.S. Guyt for legal work which enabled the sharing of Hoek's study in America.

Here at home, special thanks must go to my friend Don Wynschenk, who translated Hoek's work from Dutch to English and to typist Alice Christensen for her manuscript work.

Appreciation is expressed for the photographic work of Ed Lambrecht of Montville, CT and to Bill Lessig for the use of Connecticut College facilities, and as always to my friends, John Kowalski and former U.S National Coach, Walt Chyzowych who gave me the opportunity to work as a USSF Staff Coach and MISL Referee-in-Chief.

A special thank you is offered to Kevin Driscoll of Phoenix Press for his guidance and advice on many projects, but none so technical and complicated in detail as this work.

Sincere appreciation is extended to my wife, Barbara, for her encouragement and fortitude in multifarious assignments ranging from proof-reading, re-typing and finding the right word to being, along with our daughters, Colette and Janine, the motivation and reason for it all.

Finally to the American goalkeepers and their coaches, thank you for your hard work, quest for knowledge and sincere dedication to excellence at the position of goalkeeper. It has been your attitude and perserverance which in the end has earned a text dedicated to you and your performance. SO NOW YOU ARE A GOALKEEPER - Go to it!

Author's Note: The authors recognize that some forty percent of all soccer players are women and have written this text with that understanding. However, in an effort to make literary sense and simplify the reading we have chosen to refer to the goalkeeper and coach in masculine terms.

Index

Introduction

Certainly the goalkeeper is becoming increasingly considered as one of the eleven players on a soccer team, and not as much as an outsider although by nature, as an individualist he is still a loner.

The goalkeeper is still the only player with special playing privileges within his own penalty area. He distinguishes himself by wearing special colors and protective gear and for the most part plays in the worse area of the field often *"miles away"* from the game's action.

Upon the giving up of a goal the goalkeeper is at the center of disappointment, is often to blame whether rightfully or not and yet is most often the player furtherest away during the celebration when a goal is scored by his team. Often he must celebrate by himself.

In preparing for a match there is little the goalkeeper can do to influence the play of his counterpart who will be at the other end of the field. This is greatly unlike the rest of the team and the players concerned with man to man marking and zone coverage with particular emphasis on certain players. The goalkeeper can be only concerned about his job, and the traditional hand shake of opposing goalkeepers prior to the start of a game is a symbol of the understanding that each has of the job to be done. This hand shake is not taken lightly, there is nothing but seriousness about the tasks at hand.

Realizing that the goalkeeper is different is the first step toward effective coaching of goalkeepers. But there are still coaches who do not recognize that the goalkeeper by the nature of his position has earned the right to be coached with a different point of view. Their practices reflect this lack of understanding which has as its root cause a lack of knowledge.

There have been many textbooks written by former field players who are now coaching that have included chapters and sections on goalkeeping. And of course, many of the world's famous goalkeepers have taken the opportunity to share some of their playing expertise and experiences through picture books with narrative designed to increase loyalty and fan appreciation.

By combining the still fresh experiences of an active goalkeeper with coaching credentials in the person of Frans Hoek with the 25 years experience in dealing with goalkeepers at every level of the American game in the person of Joe Machnik, "So Now You Are A Goalkeeper" is an attempt to finally treat the subject of goalkeeping in its rightful place and with the proper point of view.

"So Now You Are A Goalkeeper" is written not only for the goalkeeper and his coach, but with the field player and spectator also in mind. Its purpose is to increase understanding which will allow for the betterment of play. While the text is very thorough, the authors recognize that as it is being read, new coaching ideas, goalkeeping tips and training methods are being developed.

In addition, questions may be answered through the No. 1 Goalkeeper's Camp by writing to P.O. Box 107, Branford, CT 06405; Phone 1-800-MACHNIK.

So Now You are a Goalkeeper

Chapter One

Background

1. Psychological Factors

1.1. The Relationship between the Goalkeeper and Coach

Interpersonal relationships have a great deal to do with the success of the goalkeeper. Getting together over a soft drink or coffee for small talk about the "keeper's" hobbies, as well as, his job is very important to the well being of the keeper. The coach will often need patience, confidence and the ability to show knowledge about the tasks and responsibilities of the goalkeeper in order to develop the optimal in companionship which is often necessary to achieve the best playing results. Goalkeepers are often loners, pure individualists with a variety of tasks within a team. The goalkeeper may have to be pampered a bit or otherwise treated with a slightly different approach or level of attention than the individual field player.

It would be the ideal situation for the coach to get completely involved with goalkeeping and from that the goalkeeper's work excels. In most cases this is impossible, hense the emergence in some teams and programs of the specific goalkeeper coach. This coach fully realizes what the goalkeeper needs and wants and also recognizes the goalkeeper's human capabilities, as well as, the performance under the crossbar. Upon this foundation the coach can base the training program using match performance as the barometer. The game will illustrate to the knowledgeable coach the strengths and weaknesses of the goalkeeper and the coach's full understanding of the goalkeeper's success and failure. Patience is thoroughly tested in this process, developing a competent goalkeeper is a long drawn out affair until the goalkeeper is able to play at 100% of potential. Good goalkeepers are not developed in a single day or practice, and no coach has this ability.

The coach must have a natural feeling for the goalkeeper to be able to develop a closeness whereby the coach becomes the confidant of the goalkeeper. Through this closeness, the coach can convince the goalkeeper of things that have not been thought about or seen before. There must be specific concentrated practice sessions for the goalkeeper. After shooting or serving a ball the coach cannot have his attention drawn away from the goalkeeper by some other matter pertaining to the rest of the team. The goalkeeper cannot work without attention. The coach must not let the goalkeeper's accepted level of performance drop unless he or she is ready to accept the consequences of a poor game which the goalkeeper has dragged the coach through because proper preparation for perfect play has not been established in practice.

1.1.1. Factors which Can Hinder the Confidence of the Goalkeeper

A.   Lack of Attention - The bullying of the goalkeeper can be deadly for his form. Abuse based on lack of knowledge or limited knowledge, which views the goalkeeper principally or solely as a stopper of shots is often the cause. A solution must be found between the coach and the goalkeeper to provide meaningful practice sessions.

B.   Punishment - Training with all kinds of unimportant drills and exercises which have nothing to do with goalkeeping becomes punishment. To achieve positive results, exercises must simulate game conditions. An hour's practice session with all concentration on the goalkeeper is often not enough.

C.   Sharp Shooting - Most coaches are ex-field players and seemingly enjoy picking the corners on goalkeepers. So in an hour's practice there are the seven perfect shots and the rest miss the crossbar and post by inches. Nothing can be more demoralizing for the keeper. The purpose of training is for the keeper to get better and stronger and to develop the belief that he is impassable. He must train with shots that are just savable and work his way from there.

D.   Criticism and Praise - The goalkeeper is looking for help from the coach and the coach must realize where fault lies. Belittling the goalkeeper for mental mistakes often has negative results. Laziness on the other hand cannot be tolerated. Poor preparation is often the fault of the coach. A compliment for a good job in goal cannot hurt. Then again, when arrogance interferes with performance, the coach must pull in the reins. Knowing exactly what gets the goalkeeper up and what demoralizes him is the coach's best tool. The coach must know the goalkeeper thoroughly.

E.   Comparison to other Goalkeepers - Comparison to much better keepers often does little good. The coach should work with the goalkeeper's current level and style toward a form of perfection. Positive reinforcement through the analyzation of other goalkeeper's play may provide proper example, but as an individualist, each goalkeeper's play may provide proper example, but as an individualist, each goalkeeper must establish his own identification.

F.   Dishonest Coaching - If the coach has little knowledge of the technical and tactical elements of goalkeeping he should do everything in his or her power to attain these, rather than try to fool the goalkeeper, ad-lib or otherwise. Especially with an experienced goalkeeper the coach would often ridicule himself. The coach should try to get in goal himself during a training session or scrimmage. He should talk with the goalkeeper in honest dialogue about his own experience and question the goalkeeper about his training needs. However, the match tells all.

All of these points lead to a better underlying relationship, the foundation of good goalkeeper coaching.

1.2. The Goalkeeper on Stage

The reality of soccer is that in most cases the goalkeeper is looked upon as the leader of the defense. The entire team can be seen in a positive or negative manner as its performance is directly related to how well the goalkeeper holds himself in goal. The keeper must show confidence. He must overcome fear —the three fears of goalkeepers being the fear of failure, the fear of embarrassment, and the fear of injury. If fear cannot be overcome the goalkeeper must do well to hide that fear as much as possible. The leader of the defense is on stage, there can be no "stage fright" and the goalkeeper must present himself as self-assured and confident.

When the keeper gets too involved with what else is happening on the field, this often causes irritation with the rest of the squad. When direction *must* be given to the defense, it must be done loudly and clearly. The keeper must keep himself busy with the defensive tactics at hand. Defense is often a total team effort, so all players are dependent on the performance of the keeper. The working relationship between the goalkeeper and the team's defensive effort are best judged by the goals against. The entire team will be presented in a stronger posture with the feeling that everything in the back is secure if the goalkeeper is able to:

1. appear confident and sure;
2. give good directions.

However, the following points could be fatal:

1. nervous and unsure posture (not reassuring);
2. close-mouthedness — causing mistakes or misunderstanding;
3. too much talking.

These often cause havoc in the team. A confident and competent goalkeeper who properly leads and directs the team's defensive effort strengthens the morale of the team, and in addition, worries the opposition.

1.3. Superstition

A mascot in goal. The old red shirt, a sweater, a certain place in the locker room, a parrot or even an old piece of cloth. Superstition has its place in the world of sports and the superstitious goalkeeper also belongs.

What do we understand superstition to be? For sure, it is the creation of a sign or symbol that influences in a positive way. This often spiritual influence plays a role of great importance in many athletes running the gamut from the mentally toughest to the most physically weak.

It would be ridiculous for the coach to view a superstition as a form of weakness. Certainly, the goalkeeper has a much stronger feeling toward the superstition than any casual observer. The superstition should never get between the goalkeeper and the coach. What ever the superstition or mascot in goal, as long as it strengthens the keeper, this will also do the same for his performance and will be good for the team as well. When the superstition gets broken or is tested unnecessarily, it may also test the athlete's self-confidence.

Some examples of goalkeeper superstitions with game preparation are:
1. an exact time period for sleep;
2. the keeping of an exact life-style;
3. dressing in uniform in exact order;
4. the exact place in the locker room;
5. where massage is given, the exact order of massage;
6. certain clothing—certain color;
7. a mascot;
8. hanging around a certain player;
9. a prayer.

1.4. The Reserve or Substitute Goalkeeper

In contrast to other players, there is only one place for the keeper and that is in goal. Therefore, for the reserve goalkeeper, there is only one focal point for his concentration and to which the coach must pay attention, this is under the crossbar. For the back-up goalkeeper, there is only one chance to play; as soon as the so called first choice disappears. This may happen through:
1. loss of form;
2. injury;
3. other problems.

In the case that this does not happen, then the reserve goalkeeper has to be satisfied with taking his place on the bench. When we categorize the reserve goalkeeper, we cover four particular personalities:
1. The ambitious one - coming from the youth, junior varsity, or freshman class. This goalkeeper has no real experience at the new level and, therefore, cannot claim anything.
2. The keeper recovering from injury who wants to recover his starting position. If the rehabilitation is prompt and his former performance cannot be matched by his replacement, then there are few problems. If the substitute is doing well, then the comeback becomes more difficult. The result is often an upset goalkeeper which the coach must constantly reckon with.
3. The passed-up goalkeeper, most often the result of getting out of shape, losing form or the much-improved reserve goalkeeper. This goalkeeper often causes uncomfortable situations due to his own frustrations which may cause problems for the coach.
4. The complacent reserve. This goalkeeper almost never causes a problem and is happy about his place on the bench.

For the coach, it is important to know with which of these four personalities he is dealing with, especially to take full advantage of the situation. The coach must make the back-up keeper believe that he is a definite part of the entire team. The coach must keep in mind that the back-up keeper is someone who has love for his sport and is someone who has a need to be treated equally with the first goalkeeper. This must be remembered in training, for game preparation, and in meetings or conferences. It now becomes the task of the coach to make the choice between the two goalkeepers; only one can play. This choice is fairly easy if the class of performance between the goalkeepers is very obvious, more difficult if the difference between the two is small.

The choice in goalkeepers must be with the team, the possible result and the effect of each goalkeeper on team performance. The routine of the team may be the deciding factor, or the strengths and weaknesses of each goalkeeper when placed against the scouting report on the opposition. Is one goalkeeper stronger in the air, better reading the through pass, or perhaps better on long range shots? With younger vs. older goalkeepers, we are often deciding between match experience (savy) and aggressive demonstrative actions based on inaccurate decision making. Perhaps distribution factors are the key to this decision.

Usually goal experience gives the choice to the older goalkeeper. Once this choice is made, it is best for the coach to explain why in an honest fashion. It has been proven that playing one goalkeeper against the other often leads to bringing down the level of play of both. Changing goalkeepers regularly back and forth especially when one makes a mistake goes against the conditioning of both, breaks confidence and often loses games. Except for indoor soccer where the physical and mental demand are much greater, it is better to fully give confidence to one goalkeeper and deal with the personality of the goalkeeper chosen to be the reserve.

The reserve goalkeeper must be kept match fit, however, and the feeling must be kept alive that he is a total part of the team. The back-up keeper should be used in practice games or exhibitions that might be played during the regular season, especially if the starting keeper has a good fitness level or might, in fact, deserve a rest. At all times the coach must know:

1. what is the attitude of the reserve goalkeeper;
2. to give the reserve goalkeeper confidence;
3. to make an honest choice between the first and second goalkeeper and take time to give reasons for this choice;
4. to give both equal respect;
5. that he is dealing with a reserve goalkeeper, not a changeable goalkeeper.

1.5. Concentration and Anticipation

The goalkeeper concentrates for the full 90 minutes, even though the ball may be played as few as five or six times per game. The goalkeeper must live with everything that happens on the field although not externally show over-concern to his teammates and opponents. He must keep the space between himself and the last defender small enough that he can win that space when a ball is played into the space in the form of a through pass or cross. He must be the sweeper for the sweeper.

Quick decisions based upon proper reading of the game (anticipation), will come from the goalkeeper who properly positions himself in accordance with every situation at hand. When the ball is in the far third of the field the goalkeeper should play about 16 to 18 yards out from the goal-line. There is no safety between the posts. As the ball comes closer; the goalkeeper systematically retreats except, for example, when the situation demands an interception and the goalkeeper must move forward. There are no set positions, everything is relative to the ball; the placement of the players, the strengths of the players and the strengths of the goalkeeper. The goalkeeper must always seek to take part in the play and bring himself as close to the play as possible except in those situations that by doing so he would be taking an unnecessary risk that may favor the opponent.

Therefore, communication with the last defender is extremely important, especially regarding distances and space. The coach should hesitate in thinking about frequent substitutions in these two vital positions.

2. External Factors

2.1. Goalkeeping Uniforms

An old sweater knitted by grandma, a roomy pull-over vest, boots with steel toes and spit in the hands, this characterized the goalkeeper of yesterday. However, in just the last few years, there has been tremendous development in the area of goalkeeping uniforms and equipment.

Today, there are many possibilities for the goalkeeper to look his best. And while looking good is part of the idea, the goalkeeper nevertheless must feel good in his uniform. The uniform must be functional for the position, as well as, make an impression on the opponent.

The importance of the goalkeeper's shirt is often underestimated. The choice of color, regardless of superstition has many variables which relate to certain situations. A yellow colored shirt, for example, has advantages for games played at night, as far as the light reflection is concerned. Studies have shown that brightly colored shirts (yellow or orange) can influence the actions of attacking players. During a lvl breakaway against the goalkeeper, the forward with his head down, sees the shadow of the goalkeeper caused by light reflected by the brightly colored jersey and the first reaction of the forward is often a shot directly into the shadow and a save for the keeper.

Of course, this shadow effect is less important during day games, when the choice of color might best be decided by the differentiation between the colors worn by the competing teams. Yellow, blue, green and silver-grey seem to be the most chosen and neutral colors. In any case, it is best for the goalkeeper to always have two distinctly different colored jerseys at all times.

With two jerseys the chance of having the same color as the opponent is nullified and, of course, in bad weather the second clean and dry shirt could be changed into at half-time.

Considerable attention is being directed to the safety aspects of the goalkeeper's jersey. The modern goalkeeper's jersey has several layers of foam rubber padding in the area of the elbows. There are varied opinions on these elbow pads, and flexibility is the main concern as movement must not be restricted, and the pad must be sewn in properly, so that it stays in the area of the elbow. Regardless, on frozen fields and indoors, elbow padding is essential. Some top indoor goalkeepers wear conventional ice-hockey elbow pads under their goalkeeper's jersey to afford extra protection (see Illust. 1).

Next to the shirt, goalkeeping shorts rank in importance and considerable improvements have been made in the last several years. There are several styles including the long, narrow so-called "Bermuda" shorts. Today these shorts are very popular as they provide extra warmth through the long length of the leg muscles and further protect the leg from irritating scrapes and "raspberries," the bane of all goalkeepers.

The highest quality goalkeeper shorts have removable padded inserts which vary in thickness according to the goalkeeper's needs. During wet weather these pads can pick up quite a bit of moisture and mud, becoming heavy and restrictive to the goalkeeper and should be changed at half-time. Often overlooked in the shirt/short combination is the length of the shirt and the goalkeeper's ability to keep it tucked inside the shorts so that in diving and sliding saves the shirt will not ride up exposing bare skin to the ground in the area of the upper side and back.

The goalkeeper's socks are usually no different from the rest of the squad, and are not considered to provide a special advantage of any kind. Goalkeepers should always train in long socks and keep their socks up during games for aesthetic, as well as safety considerations. Socks which are able to be held up properly will not be distracting to the goalkeeper during the taking of goalkicks or punts.

While the shirts, shorts and socks are the standard equipment for all goalkeepers, protective equipment has now become the order of the day. The sewn-in elbow pad has practically eliminated the old elbow pad, except for indoors and on extremely hard fields, or after an injury. Elbow pads provide protection, but have the disadvantage of restricting movement. Knee pads have also similarly disappeared, although certain styles with broad elastic bands in both top and bottom, thus limiting the distracting nuisance of movements of the pad, have remained in use for goalkeepers who need protection because of previous injury or field conditions and who still wish to wear short pants instead of the longer knicker or long pants.

Long pants (see Illust. 2) are becoming increasingly more popular and are a must for astro-turf, indoors, or fields with worn-out goal areas. In addition to providing protection, long pants and knickers (see Illust. 3) help eliminate the third and sometimes most important fear of goalkeepers: the fear of injury. Nothing is more irritating than the field or rug burns which take so long to heal and require proper dressing to prevent sticking to clothes, and even bed sheets. The modern long pants and knickers have hip and knee padding and the goalkeeper should experiment with replaceable padding and thicker padding as conditions require.

The laws of the game have recently changed to require the mandatory use of shin guards for all players, including goalkeepers. As the role of the goalkeeper continues to change, requiring more soccer playing skills and use of the feet, it was only a matter of time before goalkeepers who were accustomed to playing without shin guards voluntarily made this change. Today's modern shin protector is light and non-restrictive, and the goalkeeper is not restricted in any way by its use. (see Illust. 4)

Goalkeepers must always consider safety and the goalkeeper coach must realize that to properly train a goalkeeper, he must require the constant exposure of the goalkeeper to the dangerous situations of each game. While needing to expose the goalkeeper to such danger, the coach must do everything to protect the goalkeeper from needless injury, especially in practice. A full dress uniform for each practice session is a step in that direction.

2.2 Footwear

Regardless of the level of play, from the lowest amateur to the pros, there is one moment of play whereby the game can be decided by the footwear of the goalkeeper.

Probably the most famous "slip" of recent history was Cameroon's fine goalkeeper, Thomas N'Kono, losing his footing in the 1984 World Cup game against Italy. Stretching to reach a lobbing shot over his right shoulder, N'Kono lost his footing and fell as a savable ball landed in the back of the net. This "slip" enabled Italy to advance to the next round and eliminated Cameroon. This "slip" put Italy through to the quarter finals where they began improved play and led to their eventual championship title. Just one slip.

Illustration 1.   Typical goalkeeper's shirt with sewn-in padded elbow and shoulders.

Illustration 2.   Long pants with sewn-in hip pads and stirrups to keep pants stretched in shoe preventing ride-up.

Illustration 3.   Typical shin guards.

Illustraion 4.   Goalkeeper's Warm-Up Suit (by Alix).

Every goalkeeper should have a pair of shoes with screw-in aluminum studs of 16mm length. These cleats work best on soft fields and the typical chewed-up front of the goal area.

The goalkeeper may prevent exposure to knee-injury caused by the "sticking in" of the front cleats by reducing their length to 14mm. In any event, it is the aluminum stud which has proven to provide the best grip of the ground.

However, on frozen fields, or fields with no grass, the flat soled shoe or shoe with multiple studs is best used. If cleats are worn on these fields, it is good to have them hollowed-out near the top to provide better grip.

While a specific shoe for the goalkeeper has yet to be made, today's goalkeeper must realize the necessity to own several different kinds of shoes and to have these ready at a moment's notice as field conditions change during each game and especially at each end of the field.

In regard to shoe laces, since most goalkicking and goal-punting (drop or volley kicks) are taken with the instep, the goalkeeper should avoid the tying of a bulky knot or any other unevenness with the shoe laces on the instep or top of the shoe. The knot can easily be tied to the side or not too tightly at the ankle.

Illustration 5.   A top quality soccer shoe with full grain leather upper, nylex lining, and six stud outsole (Alix Classic).

2.3 Goalkeeper Gloves

The grip on the ball is determined by the gloves and the need for a better grip has been caused by the emergence of the synthetic ball which becomes slippery to the bare hand. In the days of the pure leather ball, a little spit in the hands provided a sure grip and the English glove with the paddle-tennis (Ping-Pong) surface provided a good grip on the wet leather ball which often absorbed moisture and became very heavy.

But while water proofing the ball has helped the field players, as the ball stays the same weight throughout the game, it has hindered the goalkeeper.

As the goalkeeper is the only player in the game of soccer allowed to use his hands, his gloves are an unquestioned necessity. In fact, gloves are as important to the goalkeeper as shoes are to his teammates.

Goalkeeper gloves and the scientific research which now goes into the design of each pair are a relatively new phenomenon. It has been reported (Carli 1985) that the Spanish goalkeeper Zamora wore gloves in the 1930's. Surely these gloves were used solely to keep his hands warm or dry in unpleasant playing conditions, as these gloves could only have been made of cotton or leather.

In 1974, the German goalkeeper Sepp Maier wore specifically designed goalkeeper gloves with a smooth palm, which made performance easier in either wet or dry conditions ... and so began the appearance of goalkeeper gloves as a technical aid regardless of the playing circumstances. Since then there has been a technological evolution in palm designs, cosmetics, as well as the addition of the velcro wrist fastener. Because of these recent innovations goalkeeper gloves today are an essential equipment item for all goalkeepers at every level of play.

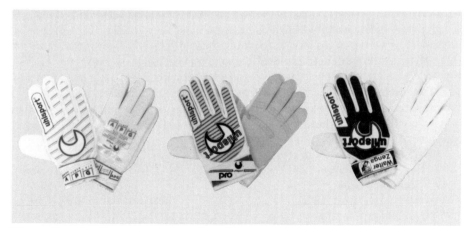

Illustration 6.   Some examples of goalkeepers gloves.

In choosing the correct model for you, two key factors must be considered: the weather and field conditions (including indoor soccer) you expect to encounter, and the level of play you can reasonably expect to reach with this particular pair of gloves. Some of the less elaborate models are designed for training where durability is more important that absolute grip or cosmetic design. Similarly the Youth Player, whose skill and athletic ability is still developing, is better off using a more economical glove as it better suits his current level of proficiency. The more developed high school, college, or professional will choose the top models for match play to get maximum grip and comfort with the velcro strap designs. This player is interested in top performances and quality.

Recent innovations include the use of Gortex material to provide the ultimate in warmth and the APG (Advanced Power Grip) surface which promises 70% greater catching and holding qualities than any glove previously made.

In choosing gloves for particular weather and field conditions, keep in mind that as a general rule wet weather gloves have a softer palm surface for maximum gripping while dry weather and indoor gloves are harder and have somewhat less grip but absorb ball-shock better. Check the "Recommended usage" table on the glove packaging or in the latest catalog to be certain of that particular model's optimal usage.

Picking the correct size to wear is obviously vital. American athletes tend to prefer to wear sports equipment (shoes, clothing, etc.) tight to the body. Conversely it is much better to choose a goalkeeper glove size one-half to one full size larger—so that it fits loosely on the hand. This allows the glove to "give" when it receives the ball allowing for more shock-absorption and less wear in the palm area. A larger glove also allows for more glove surface on the ball — increasing gripping power.

Proper maintenance of your gloves can increase their useful life considerably. After a match in very wet conditions it is important to allow the gloves to drip-dry naturally. If the gloves becomes very muddy they can be hand washed in cold water using a very weak concentration of detergent. Again allow them to drip-dry. Never attempt to dry them in a dryer, in front of a heater or fire, or in direct sunlight— this will make the palm hard and brittle. In the normal usage of goalkeeper gloves, the palm surface will show signs of wear. In fact, gloves that are slightly worn will have the greatest grip — many top goalkeepers will rub their hands together when breaking in a new pair. Of course the best way to ensure longer glove life is to use proper goalkeeping technique. That, more than even your gloves, will be the measure of your success as a goalkeeper.

2.4 Protection from the Sun

Depending upon climatic conditions, the height of the sun, the time of the year, the lay-out of the field, there will be times where the goalkeeper must consider the prevention of the momentary blindness that comes with a concentrated look into the sun. In addition, a low sun at the opposite end of the field may cause a stressful situation for the goalkeeper with no opportunity for resting the eyes.

Illustration 7.   Some further examples of goalkeeping gloves.

Throughout history, goalkeepers have used sun visors, see-through sun visors, eye-black, and caps. The goalkeeper's cap has the advantage of providing a restful atmosphere for the eyes in blinding situations while being able to be knocked off in emergencies.

Visors are sometimes more cumbersome, but there are see-through visors which allow for vision of the ball to be maintained even while looking up at the ball in the sun.

Many goalkeepers prefer to go capless and practice their ability to look at a ball in the sun through their eye-lashes thus preventing the momentary blindness and the possible break in concentration having to deal with a cap, as well as the change that comes from the protected view of the cap or visor and the sudden reality of having to look past that protection to the top, left, right or even backward.

2.5   *The Goalkeeper's Equipment Bag* (Illust. 7B, page 17)

The following is a list of minimum equipment from the available extensive assortment that all goalkeepers must keep in their equipment bag to be adequately and thoroughly prepared for any goalkeeping situation:
1.   Two goalkeeper jerseys of different color — to preclude the possibility of conflict with the colors of the opponent and also to provide a clean, dry jersey at half-time on wet days.

2. Shorts — light weight unpadded shorts for that perfect field, padded shorts for hard fields, long padded shorts (Bermuda style) for extra warmth and protection. Remember extra removable pads as inserts.
3. Long pants and/or knickers for astro-turf, indoors, extremely cold days, extremely abrasive field conditions.
4. Long socks with several strips of cloth as ties (avoid rubber bands or elastics which might cut circulation, cause cramps or numbness of the feet) to hold socks up.
5. Suitable shoes for field conditions.
6. Towel.
7. Under garments.
8. Sweat suit — essential for warming up.

In addition to the above minimum requirements, the following seem necessary:
1. Sun visor or cap;
2. Elbow pads;
3. Knee pads;
4. Extra socks;
5. Extra shorts or pants;
6. Extra pair of shoes — back-up pair in case game pair becomes damaged;
7. Extra shoe laces;
8. Extra cleats and cleat pliers or wrench;
9. Shin guards;
10. Wraps for ankle and tape for care of possible injury — ace bandage;
11. Rain jacket and rain pants for warming up in wet weather;
12. Several pair of gloves with various grips;
13. Glove bag to protect gloves from abuse and provide for further proper care.

2.6 Tips for Inclement Weather

Training or playing in inclement weather provide unique problems for the goalkeeper. Regarding long pants; knickers or pants with stirrups will prevent the lower pants leg from becoming water-logged, heavy or sloppy, causing the pants to sag. For practice, pants may be held by:
1. suspenders;
2. rope or cord through the waist (tie string);
3. rope around the pants;
4. shorts over the pants.

Rain pants will not last long in any practice situation, hense the need for being prepared to keep pants up on a wet practice field.

Today, much is being made of water repellent materials, but cotton jerseys offer the most resistance to the ball. A thermal jersey or rain jacket provides a dangerously slippery surface for the ball; however, the cotton jersey absorbs water and becomes heavy.

The goalkeeper must also concern himself with the absorption of his own body perspiration and it often becomes necessary to wear a long t-shirt under the water repellent or water resistant goalkeeping jersey in order for perspiration to be absorbed. The long t-shirt tucked into the underwear will also provide further protection to the bare skin in situations where the shirt might rise up or the shorts or pants become lowered in a diving maneuver or save.

2.7 Field and Weather Conditions

The goalkeeper must practice in all field and weather conditions in order not to be surprised by any element in which he may be forced to play. The following conditions are most treacherous.

1. Wind — Very undependable ... The goalkeeper must constantly be aware of changes and swirls and study the wind both in the warm-up and at the start of the second half as to its effect on the ball ... does the wind hold up the ball or cause it to shoot by? What is the effect of the wind on crosses and corner kicks?
2. Sun — Sun protection has been reviewed on page 13.
3. Slippery Field — The ball will speed up and skip like a flat rock thrown on the surface of a smooth body of water. The goalkeeper must be ready for this strange bounce and prevent rebounds and embarrassments on relatively easy shots.
4. Puddles — Upon one occasion the ball may be held up by the puddle, on another it may skip (speed and treachery are the difference). The goalkeeper must familiarize himself with all puddles, get to know the worst places and be prepared to dive head-long into a puddle to get a stationary ball that is still in play.
5. Solid Frozen Field — Strange bounces and difficult footing make these conditions awful for the keeper when added to his concern for injury. Courage is important and the warm-up is the best guide for the keeper, don't think ... just get the job done!
6. Frozen Field covered with Snow — Diving may be a little easier, depending upon the depth of the snow, footing may also be improved. The ball will react differently and the goalkeeper will need to study changes in the field (snow) caused by slide tackles, fallen bodies, foot prints. Be ready for anything including snow on the ball.
7. Combinations — Wind and slippery field, as well as multifarious other combinations require the goalkeeper to be aware constantly of present, as well as changing conditions.
8. Ideal Field Conditions — Semi-soft field, dry grass, no wind, sun not a problem ... "lots of luck!" Welcome to Shangri-La.

2.8   The Ball

The best ball possible, and in good condition:
1. the ball is round;
2. properly inflated;
3. proper weight;
4. not too worn.

Four to twelve balls are necessary for practice and there should be little or no difference between one ball and the next.

A bad ball in poor condition (different size, shape, weight) may easily cause injury to the goalkeeper's hand, wrist, fingers, hyperextension of the elbow.

Also, a ball in poor condition, which is difficult to hold, causes a deterioration of the confidence of the goalkeeper. Under all circumstances, the goalkeeper should train with the ball that is going to be used in the game and also test the game ball prior to the game's start (with the permission of the referee, of course — test for bounce, size, grip). The large number of practice balls (4–12) necessary for a goalkeeping training session is to minimize waiting time, thus making the practice as economical as possible.

2.9   The Height of the Goalkeeper

A crucial question for the goalkeeper is that of height. Too short? Too tall? It can seem that body type, especially height, can have a definite bearing on the way a goalkeeper functions in goal. Short goalkeepers (5'5" to 5'9") often have the advantage of:
1. quickness;
2. athletic ability (flexibility);
3. agility (violent change of direction),

but a disadvantage in:
1. dueling for high balls;
2. extended reach;
3. being vulnerable to lobs.

Often the "short" goalkeeper does not expose himself to those aspects of the game with which he has difficulty, and becomes a so-called "line-keeper," who almost never comes out of the goal to battle for high balls.

Improvement in the training of vertical jump through the "Russian Step Ladder Method" or through the use of machines such as the "Leaper" or "Jumper" may open up new avenues of performance capability for the "short" keeper. And, of course, there are always exceptions to every rule and it would be wrong to categorize all short goalkeepers as line-keepers.

Above 5'10", the "tall keeper" has the following advantages:
1. dominates on high balls;
2. great reach;

but often these disadvantages:
1. not too quick;
2. low level of flexibility (athletic ability);
3. vulnerable on low balls and ball at feet.

Just because a goalkeeper is tall tells us little about his quality. The elements of talent, training and character are important variables. There are also small goalkeepers, who play "big" or give that impression and vice versa. Nevertheless, a tall goalkeeper with athletic ability and the tools to intimidate the opponent can cut off many opportunities before they develop into serious goal-scoring chances.

Forward players who are aware of the goalkeeper's reputation as a strong boxer of the ball, and one who welcomes opportunities for aerial combat may very well decide not to take this route to goal. Now the goalkeeper can play further off his line to deal with through passes, as his height and ability to go backward discourages long range shooting or lob shots to the bar. For the coach, this goalkeeper has the tremendous advantage of simplifying defensive tactics. Now the coach can concentrate on attacking soccer and even in this regard, the taller goalkeeper with longer levers, should be able to throw, punt and take goalkicks over greater distances with accuracy.

The physical dimension of height when combined with athletic ability cannot be substituted. With small goalkeepers, especially those with limited athletic ability, the coach is faced with compensation and protection, a detriment to attacking soccer.

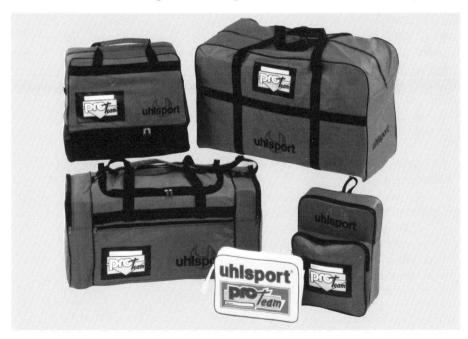

Illustration 7B. Various kinds of equipment bags and goalkeeper's glove bag.

Chapter Two

Training the Goalkeeper - General Principles

1.   Introduction

1.1.   Training Separately or as Part of the Group?
While it is possible to train the perfection of technique in goalkeeping separately and also work on the goalkeeper's fitness in this fashion, it is also very important for the goalkeeper to work with the rest of the team in the following situations:
A.   With several forms of finishing near the goal where the presence of the goalkeeper is necessary;
B.   With small-sided games with goalkeepers;
C.   With small-sided games without goalkeepers wherein the goalkeeper plays as the last player (sweeper). . .a situation which happens in the game now and then.

1.2.   When to Train the Goalkeeper?
1.   At the same time as the field players, with the special skill of a goalkeeper trainer.
2.   At a time when the field players are not training (day off - day after a game).
3.   Before practice and then include the goalkeeper in team practice.
4.   After practice - often difficult due to fatigue of other players and their desire to "go home early."
5.   In the evening - especially when night games are part of the regular schedule.
6.   On rainy days - to simulate actual field conditions on game days.

1.3.   How Long to Practice and How Often?
Depending on the circumstances, of course, the following are variables to be considered:
—   the period of training (general preparation, pre-season, specific preparation for opponents, training between games - mid season - off season);
—   the intensity of the practice;
—   the other responsibilities of the goalkeeper i.e., high school student, college student, part-time laborer, evening employment, marital and family considerations, health of the goalkeeper;
—   the status of the goalkeeper [level of play];
A.   amateur;
B.   apprentice or reserve;
C.   semi-professional;
D.   professional.

— the nature and philosophy of the high school or college program (ranging from recreational to win oriented);

— the aspirations of the goalkeeper and/or his coach.

At the very minimum, the goalkeeper needs specific training at least twice a week at status A, three times a week at status B and four times a week at status C.

The length of the training session depends upon:

— the intensity;

— the make-up of the goalkeeper (preference to short, but heavy practice as opposed to longer light practice);

— most importantly the determination of what is necessary to improve the goalkeeper's play or prepare him for the next game and opponent;

— in any event it seems that specific goalkeeping practice sessions are never shorter than a half hour or longer than one hour.

2.   The Contents of A Practice Session

A typical specific goalkeeper training session consists of:

    A.   a warm-up period;

    B.   a central core;

    C.   a closing.

A.   The warm-up (approximately 15 minutes). The objective of the warm-up is to physically and mentally prepare the goalkeeper for the rigors to follow. Always begin with walking, then a light jog to raise the blood circulation, followed by static stretching, specifically those muscles stressed in the techniques of goalkeeping. Groin, ham strings, back, neck, shoulder - the chance for injury is very high if the body has not been stretched to the point to which the practice session will take it.

A typical warm-up:

— always begin with walking easy;

— then stretch exercises;

— increase the pace of the walk and several jogs;

— walking in different directions and with various styles. . .side step left and right, backward;

— restful jumping;

— several 50 yard sprints;

— several more intense shorter sprints;

— remember to stretch in between each station and let the body tell you which area needs to be stretched more than another.

Thereafter, the warm-up is done with the ball:

— balls are played to the keeper so that he may catch and react without falling. Balls are at first played low - on the ground and up until the goalkeeper must jump to save the high shot above his head.

— finally as part of the warm-up the goalkeeper should be built up to the falling stage (see falling, page 73).

B. The core training takes about 30 minutes. It is here that the coach deals specifically with:

a. technique;

b. tactics;

c. conditioning;

d. any combination of the above three.

It is important that there is time for concentration and hard work, which may be interrupted now and then with some exercises done at a relaxed pace.

C. Closing. Many exercises are useful:

— The coach or team shoots 10 balls from the edge of the penalty area and the keeper calls the number of saves.

— If three of ten shots score the practice is over, or any variation.

— If the goalkeeper saves all ten the practice is over.

— As a warm-down the goalkeeper can walk, jog and then engage in more static stretching especially to bring "healing blood" to the injured areas (bumps and bruises of the day).

3.   A Means to Evaluation

The coach may use this evaluation chart to vary his drills and training methods in order to get a full view of the strengths and weaknesses of the goalkeeper.

If this chart is shared with goalkeeper it may become an excellent basis for motivation toward a yearly plan and to set-up training sessions accordingly. This formula may also be used to scout goalkeepers.

Name: _____

Address: _____

Birthplace: _____ Telephone: _____

School: _____ Club: _____

Occupation: _____

The occasion of the game (site-level-opponents) _____

_____ Date: _____

The body-build of the goalkeeper:

Body length:	
Use of body in drills:	*a. good* *b. fair* *c. poor*

Defending portion of the body (ball within range).

With or without steps forward, side ways or backward.				
	Good	Fair	Poor	No. of Times
1. Pick ups.				
2. Saves - picking out of the air.				
3. Flicking over.				
4. Boxing - a. with one fist. b. with two fists.				

To the side of the body/with or without dive or steps.				
	Good	Fair	Poor	No. of Times
5. Falling or diving saves (catch).				
6. Falling or diving saves (boxing): a. one fist; b. two fists.				
7. Dive at the feet.				
8. Slide at the feet.				
9. Catching crosses.				
10. Boxing crosses: a. one fist; b. two fists.				

Out side of the penalty area.				
	Good	Fair	Poor	No. of Times
11. Playing the ball with the feet.				
12. Playing the ball with head.				
13. Tackling.				

Attacking Role

	Good	Fair	Poor	No. of Times
14. Goalkicks: a. short; b. long.				
15. Punting from hand.				
16. Throwing: a. bowling; b. underhand; c. overhand sling (side arm); d. overhand pitch (baseball throw).				

Tactical Realm

	Good	Fair	Poor
17. Positioning in goal-angle play.			
18. Causing problems for the opposition.			
19. Accuracy and quickness of working the ball away once in possession.			
20. Timing and reading the game.			

Leadership Abilities

	Good	Fair	Poor
21. Leadership and Directions to teammates during: a. corner kicks; b. free kicks; c. during play; d. other restarts.			

The Goalkeeping Personality

	Good	Fair	Poor
1. Relationship to the group: a. teamates; b. coach; c. leadership.			
2. Personality during the game: a. towards referee; b. teammates; c. opposition.			
3. Can the goalkeeper deal with: a. body contact with opponents; b. taking orders from team-mates and leader.			
4. How does he act after: a. a lost game; b. winning			

4.   Yearly Plan for Goalkeeper Training

For purposes of the yearly plan we may consider the rough classification of goalkeepers according to:

I.   amateur;
II.   semi-pro or top amateur;
III.   full professional.

The serious high school or college goalkeeper falls into a combination of category II and III depending upon the emphasis placed on winning in the particular program.

Generally speaking, there are four periods of goalkeeper training as far as the above three classifications are concerned:

A.   the transition phase   (from off-season to readiness)
B.   general preparation   (getting into shape)
C.   specific preparation   (getting ready to play)
D.   competition phase   (playing and staying fit).

A.   The transition phase - The period of about six weeks prior to the beginning of regular practice sessions.

The first two weeks consist of physical and mental relaxation, being divorced totally from soccer. The mind and body need rest. Getting ready for practice, the next two weeks consist of relaxing body conditioning, such as tennis, swimming, basketball, volleyball, racquet ball. The last two weeks consists of 2 to 3 long jogs per week interchanged with power exercises (weights), maintaining flexibility through static stretching throughout this period.

B.   General preparation - The idiocyncracies of the U.S. high school and college system, forces a shortening of the general preparation period during which time the goalkeeper would engage in the regular training regimen of the team, playing with the field players and in conditioning programs similar for most athletes in a variety of sports.

However, in high school and college the first regular season game often comes within two weeks of the opening of training, hense for these goalkeepers it becomes necessary to combine the last two weeks of the transition phase and the general conditioning phase so that the goalkeeper may be ready to go almost directly into the specific preparation phase.

C.   Specific preparation - Approximately two weeks (shorter in high school and college) whereby the goalkeeper must go from the general conditioning period (getting into shape) to the specific demands of his individual position (getting ready to play). All the goalkeeping tasks and skills must be brought to match readiness level. This means training to prepare:

1.   jumping strength;
    a. height
    b. sideways (diving)
    c. forward
    d. backward
2.   stomach and back muscles;

3. arm and shoulder girdle;
   a. boxing
   b. throwing
4. hand, finger muscles, catching strength;
5. movement in goal;
6. movement in front of the goal.

It is best that most exercises are done with a ball, weighted ball or medicine ball.

Thereafter, the technical and tactical aspects of goalkeeping must be trained. This may be done through recognizing the various functions of the goalkeeper in the game and developing match situations whereby the technical functions and tactical functions may be rehearsed. The goalkeeper takes part in full practice game situations and match condition games such as 6v4 and the ever popular 4v4 with 4 waiting whereby Team A plays against Team B to one goal with the goalkeeper. As soon as A loses the ball and B recovers, then B immediately is on attack. Team C waiting behind the goal replaces the team scored upon keeping intensity high. In 15 minutes, the goalkeeper is exposed to most live game situations, and has "played" about four full games.

D. The competition phase - When the season starts, most professional teams play games once a week. High school and college teams play an average of twice a week, but there are times when three games are played in a seven day period.

During this period, it must be realized that the intensity of training is directly related to the pressure of the games both past and future. The goalkeeper must always have enough energy left to play the games. However, if the keeper relies only on the game to keep fit, he may lose real match fitness after a string of easy, less active games. The keeper must always be fit enough to execute the most difficult save in the game's closing moments or in overtime.

I. Amateur Goalkeeper - Training Twice per Week.

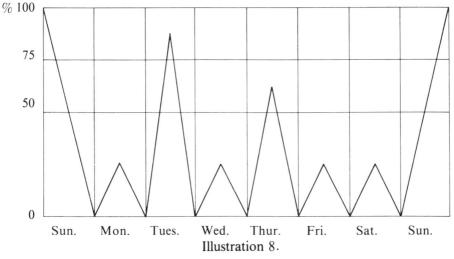

Illustration 8.

25

At the amateur level with training twice per week the player has activities other than soccer, hense the curve takes on some percentages on Monday, Wednesday, Friday and Saturday, as well as, the Tuesday and Thursday training session.

II. The "semi-pro or top amateur" as far as training 4 periods per week.

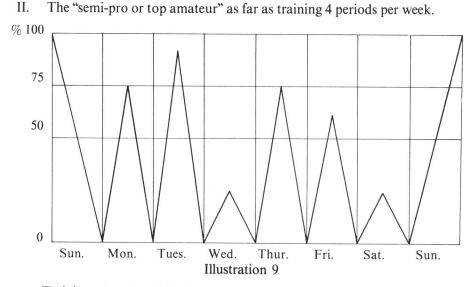

Illustration 9

Training takes place Monday, Tuesday, Thursday and Friday. Wednesday and Saturday are free.

III. The full professional - As much as a single training session on Monday, double sessions on Tuesday and Thursday, and a single session on Friday. Wednesday and Saturday are free..

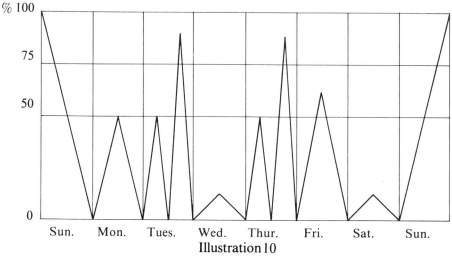

Illustration 10

Wednesday and Saturday are free, Tuesday and Thursday about 90%, Monday about 50% and Friday about 70%. In the double sessions, there is specific goalkeeping training for the 90% and the other session is with the full team.

Obviously, when two to three games are played within the seven day period, the coach must make every attempt at conversation with the goalkeeper to develop the proper balance between the necessary training rhythm required by the goalkeeper and that of the team.

Remember that winning practice is meaningless, the game is what counts.

5.   Pre-game Warm-up

The start of the game may be very difficult for the goalkeeper, the most important save opportunity may occur on the first play or in the first minute. There can be no fooling around, the warm-up for the goalkeeper must be taken very seriously.

It is important that the goalkeeper get flexible as soon as possible to prevent injuries and become mentally and physically ready to play.

The length of the warm-up varies from 12 to 25 minutes. This depends upon the field, weather conditions and the physical and psychological make-up of the goalkeeper.

The following is a characteristic chronological build-up for goalkeeper pre-game warm-up.

Preparation without the ball:
- A.   restful walking and examination for the penalty area;
- B.   loosening up the shoulder girdle, swinging the arms;
- C.   loosening up the upper legs and thighs;
- D.   loosening up the calves;
- E.   loosening up the hips by turning;
- F.   loosening up the groin;
- G.   walking and jumping with one and two leg take-offs (forward, sideways, backward);
- H.   several 50 yard sprints;   *speed is an important*
- I.   shorter sprints.   *physical requirement*

Ball warm-ups:
- A.   Shooting AT the goalkeeper by someone who understands that this warm-up period is FOR the goalkeeper and that the keeper should not be frustrated before the game begins. It is better not to have an attacker or attacking mid-fielder do this in order to see how many times or how nice they can score. Rather an assistant coach, coach, reserve goalkeeper or sweeper (he is the one who in the game must rely the most on the goalkeeper) is best for this task.

B.   Shots should be taken from 5 yards both at the goalkeeper's body and within his reach at chest, stomach, head, knee and thigh height. Do not start with so-called falling and diving exercises. The initial effort here should deal with ball feeling (hands).

C.   To play balls at jumping height — body conditioning for falling (from a sitting position, rolling and throwing the body back) then from the kneeling, squatting, and standing positions.

D.   In the goal, repeating the above to get the feel and familiarity with the goal.

E.   Shooting from the penalty-spot out to the edge of the penalty area. The keeper should "just about" be able to reach everything. Moving balls should be shot so that the keeper is constantly adjusting his position and angle play. While this is going on the goalkeeper should be distributing the saved balls by means of throw, drop-kick and punt to the exact point at the feet of the shooters and players at mid-field.

F.   Crossed balls. . .short crosses from the goal-line between the goal and the edge of the penalty area and long crosses from each touch line and corner spot — eventually with a player jumping at the goalkeeper.

G.   Full shots from the edge of the penalty area — be sure that the goalkeeper finishes with a good save which is important for the goalkeeper's mental state.

Each goalkeeper must decide for himself which series of warm-ups best prepares him for the game. In time a warm-up routine is developed and any deviation from that routine usually unsettles the goalkeeper.

Even for "friendly" or less important games, the goalkeeper must take the warm-up period seriously. It is often the case that when the goalkeeper uses a less serious or less concentrated warm-up than he is accustomed to, it is indeed that game where he gets injured or begins the decline in his form.

Technique

The first and most important task of the goalkeeper is to stop all balls which could wind up in the net. How he does this is really not important. Nevertheless, over the years several techniques have been developed which best decrease the chances of a goal by increasing the goalkeeper's ability to perform his task. The techniques covered in the next few sections are the ones used most often and are considered best at the present time. It must be pointed out, however, that there are certain techniques which sometimes come into play because of the particular body build of the goalkeeper or other circumstances which might prove a technique best for a colleague, but not for himself. It is the job of the coach to best know his keeper to help him train to best make a save.

1. Qualities of the goalkeeper

    A.   Those qualities which are possessed at birth:
1. courage;
2. character;
3. reaction time;

Directions for understanding the diagrams:

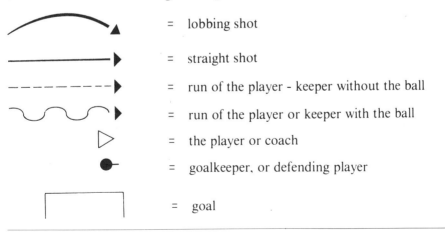

=	lobbing shot
=	straight shot
=	run of the player - keeper without the ball
=	run of the player or keeper with the ball
=	the player or coach
=	goalkeeper, or defending player
=	goal

4. athletic ability - flexibility;
5. leadership;
6. insight - reading the game - intelligence - soccer sense;
7. balance.

These qualities can be honed or sharpened, but being inborn they cannot be attributed to training. However, with experience the goalkeeper better understands game situations through the repetition of the confrontations that develop during play.

B. Qualities that are learned and improved:
1. strength;
2. coordination;
3. timing;
4. conditioning;
5. self-confidence;
6. movement skills;
7. goalkeeping techniques;
8. collegiality (teammanship);
9. decision making;
10. patience - overcoming nervousness (composure).

The coach can help the goalkeeper overcome a deficiency in these qualities.

2. Timing

What is timing? It is the use of time, between the seeing of the ball, the judgement of the speed of the ball and the coordination of the movements of the body so that at the moment of catching, boxing or distribution, there is a sense of harmony about the situation.
The most important aspects of timing are:
1. Judgement of the ball - for an estimation of good handling (at its highest point in any case, higher or quicker than the opponent — in the case of a cross or high ball in front of the goal).
2. Rhythm - The judgement of distance and the footwork to end the run at the right moment (in order to start the jump-dive).
3. Coordination - The harmonious collaboration of good technique, footwork in putting the run-jump and handling of the ball (catch, fist) into one movement.

In regard to timing, the goalkeeper must always be aware of:
A. The movement of the ball - In relation to the distance it is coming

from . . .its trajectory, as well as, speed and spin, the weather and condition of the field thus the possible condition of the ball.

    B.   Incoming players.

    C.   The covering on his teammates.

The essence of timing is its enormous importance in that every effort on the part of the goalkeeper requires proper timing or the end result is a missed opportunity to handle the ball cleanly, thus providing a real goal chance or actual goal. The need for timing occurs on:

    1.   All air balls - Balls crossed from the side, as well as, lifted up the middle, shots from the side and middle where the speed of the ball is the most important timing concern.

    2.   Balls at the far and near posts.

    3.   Balls that can be pulled back, roll backs.

    4.   Breakaway situations where timing is the key to coming out.

Catching the ball at its highest point means taking off, body totally stretched (thus also the arms) and making catching contact with the ball above or in front of the head of the opponent.

How to train for catching high balls? It is difficult for the goalkeeper to establish the proper timing, rhythm and coordination himself. It is up to the coach to provide the proper tips, cues, directions and corrections of the smallest techniques which enable the catching of the ball at the proper moment.

Drills

    1.   The goalkeeper throws the ball up and from a standing position he jumps at the ball at its highest point. Two foot take-off.

    2.   The trainer throws the ball into the air, the goalkeeper times the jump to catch at its highest possible point (coaching tip: use the crossbar as a measuring point, getting the goalkeeper to continually catch the ball at a height above the bar).

    3.   Variation - Only take two steps and take-off with one leg (see Illust. 11), again use the crossbar as a gauge.

    4.   Tossing balls above a stationary player. Goalkeeper takes a run and grabs the ball above the head of the standing player (see Illust. 12).

    5.   Stationary player now moves to interfere with the goalkeeper.

    6.   Player jumps with the goalkeeper.

    7.   Throwing of the ball from other directions (see Illust. 13).

    8.   Kicking the ball out of hand instead of throwing with various speeds, trajectory and straight shots.

    9.   The opponent at first plays:

        A.   passive;

        B.   half-active (50%);

        C.   active (90-100%).

    10.   Increase the number of opponents.

    11.   Playing the ball from further distances, the goalkeeper must grab the ball as quick as he can, at the highest possible point without permitting the ball to bounce.

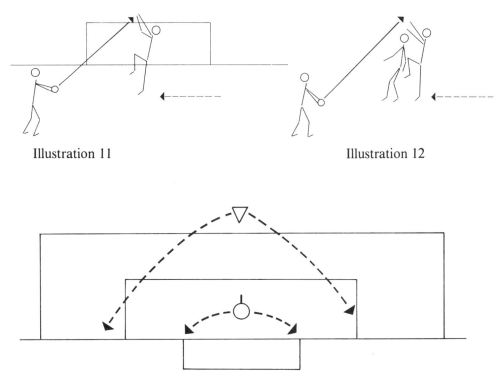

Illustration 11   Illustration 12

Illustration 13

12.   The ball may be bounced high by the trainer in the early stages of these exercises to get a match related spin and to further develop timing.

3.   Dividing the Goal Area

The goal may be divided into several different areas whereby various saving techniques might be employed.

Playing Area 1 (see Illust. 14.)

a.   Picking the ball up from the ground with or without a step forward or sideways.

b.   Ball that bounces off the ground between the ground and stomach height, bringing the ball into the stomach area with and without a step forward or sideways.

c.   Receiving the ball at stomach height, securing the ball, with or without jump, or with or without a step forward or sideways.

d.   Catching the ball at face height with or without a jump, or with or without a step forward or sideways. Ball must be brought down immediately to stomach or chest height for distribution.

Playing Area 2

a.   Catching the ball above the head, with or without a jump, with or without a step forward or backwards.

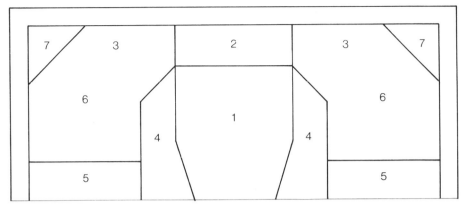

Illustration 14

b.   Tipping of the ball that cannot be caught backward with or without one or more steps backward or sideways.

Playing Area 3

a.   Catching, tipping or boxing depending upon the course and speed of the ball after one or more steps backward or sideways in taking off with or without falling or diving.

Playing Area 4

a.   Soft shots, sideways movement and similar techniques used in playing area #1.

b.   Hard shots, where there is little or no time to get the body behind the ball. Ball must be caught while falling and worked to the stomach area for protection, and secured. Be careful not to fall on the ball. Or while falling, the ball is boxed with both fists working the ball behind the goal for a corner kick or to the side of the goal, depending on the course of the ball, the speed of the shot and the conditions of the field.

Playing Area 5

a.   Diving or falling sideways, catching the ball in mid-flight toward the goal from a standing stationary position or with several steps to the side.

b.   Open hand deflection (bottom hand) around the post. The entire palm is used to re-direct the ball. The goalkeeper dives from a standing position or uses several steps to the side.

c.   Side steps and boxing of the ball around the posts or to the side of the goal.

Playing Area 6

Goalkeeper does not dive, but side steps to catch this ball at an easily playable height.

Playing Area 7

Goalkeeper dives or falls sideways to deflect the ball around the post or cross bar.

In performing the various techniques described above the goalkeeper must always take in account:

1. the angle of the shot - shots from difficult angles force a completely different view of the goal;
2. distance of the shot;
3. size of the goalkeeper;
4. style of the goalkeeper;
5. shooter's kicking foot (spin on the ball);
6. weather conditions;
7. field conditions;
8. condition of the goalkeeper's hands and ball.

4.   Training for improved Technique

4.1   The Defensive Skills

4.1.1. Ball Technique Exercises

Getting the feel of the ball:

A. Exercises with one goalkeeper and one ball.	Training Objective
1. Ball juggling - keeping the ball up with right and left instep.	Improved punting.
2. Keeping the ball up with left and right thigh.	Ball feeling.
3. Keeping the ball up with the head.	For heading when outside the penalty area.
4. Keeping the ball up with the feet, thigh, shoulders and head (juggling.)	Ball feeling.
5. Keeping the ball up using volley ball technique above the head.	Ball feeling for tipping the ball over the goal or to the side.
6. Throwing the ball up with two hands - tipping it backwards with one hand and then turning around quickly to catch the ball before it falls.	Tipping the ball, improved ball feeling both left and right, retard dizziness.
7. Repeat #6 with a jump.	
8. Playing (volleying) the ball with two fists above the head.	Improved two fisted boxing.
9. Playing (volleying) the ball with one fist - right and left, alternating.	Improved one fisted boxing.
10. Playing the ball with fists, left, right and two fists, alternating.	Improved fisting.
11. Tossing the ball with two hands, catching it behind the back.	Improved ball coordination.
12. Throwing the ball from the back, up over the head to the front.	Improved ball coordination.
13. While in a squatting position, bounce the ball off the ground using only the finger tips, left-front-right.	Finger tip strength.
14. Lying on stomach, raise upper body repeat #13 above.	Finger tip strength and stomach muscles.

B.   Exercises with two persons and one ball:
1.   partner juggling - using feet, thigh, head, shoulders;
2.   playing ball above head - volleyball style between two;
3.   one and two fisted boxing back and forth - as a defensive maneuver, height is the most important quality of a properly boxed ball;
4.   one goalkeeper tosses a lob, the other tosses the ball straight.

NOTE: The improvement of technique is best done through the recognition of faults and knowledge of methods which lead to improvement.

Every step must not be carried out A to Z. From looking at pictures, from observation, from teaching to some degree, the goalkeeper can get a clear and concise image of what is correct and what is not. The use of a video tape machine with instant slow-motion replay is a particularly good technical teaching aid.

If the goalkeeper, however, has his boxing technique down to a "T," it is useless and unnecessary to try to work to change his style or method. It is the result that counts.

But if boxing is weak, it is easily noticed in the game and through coaching can be improved. Every goalkeeper has strong and weak technical points.

The teaching of a technique could start in the middle, rather than at the beginning because the goalkeeper has advanced to a certain level, but is now stymied. When certain techniques are thoroughly under control, the coach can begin to combine the techniques such as the smooth catching of a cross followed by a drop-kick or long distance accurate throw. In this way, the coach can bring the goalkeeper from the simple to the complex.

Also, it seems that every goalkeeper has a strong side, as well as, the weaker side. It must be remembered that the strong side needs continual sharpening, while the weak side must be "over-trained." This is especially good for the goalkeeper's confidence.

In games, the goalkeeper must do his utmost to camoflague the weaker side and emphasis his strong points. Most goalkeepers are one sided as they are left or right handed.

It is difficult to break bad habits or to re-learn traits at the age of 22, it is much easier at age 10 or 12. But with practice, even the weak hand can be improved with its utilization during other activities, such as eating, writing, drinking and other sports such as offhand tennis or racquet ball.

4.1.2. Take-Offs and Positioning
The following is a short overview for the position from which the goalkeeper can best handle most balls (starting position).

1.   Stay on the balls of the feet.
2.   Bend the knees slightly - have flexibility in the hips.
3.   Arms in front of the body bent at the elbows. Hold the hands open and keep them at approximately chest height.
4.   Bending the hips forward - the upper body leans forward rather than back.
5.   Head steady - directed at the ball.

Illustration 15. Proper position for take-off.

Goalkeeper's ready position

6.   Legs spread to shoulder distance - obviously, this position is not kept throughout the game, but only those moments where the goalkeeper must ready himself for the situation.

Common Faults:
1.   Standing on heels with straight knees most easily corrected by bending the knees .
2.   Upper body too straight.
3.   Arms hanging at the sides. . .too long a distance for high balls and shots above head.
4.   Feet too close together or too far apart - the take-off takes too long because the feet need to be adjusted.

4.1.3.1 Technique for Picking Up the Ball
1.   Balls that are straight at the goalkeeper.
2.   Balls to the left or right of the goalkeeper that are near enough to him.
The following methods should be used to work at picking up these ground balls:

Illustration 16. Balls coming straight at the goalkeeper (static standing still).

Illustration 17. Balls coming straight at the goalkeeper (dynamic — with movement).

A.   Upper body leaning forward while legs are not closed completely, approximately the width of the hands, knees somewhat straight. (The ball should not be able to fit between the legs.) The ball should be scooped up with both hands to the chest - (start static as in Illust. 16).

B.   By means of several steps forward to get to the ball as quickly as possible, the goalkeeper gets to the ball coming up with bent knees and both hands scooping the ball up to the chest and stomach (dynamic - see Illust. 17).

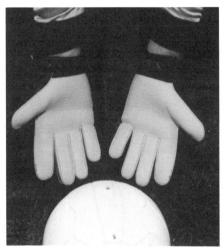

Common Faults:

1.   Legs too far apart.

2.   Hands not behind the ball, but to the side, allowing space that the ball could go through.

3.   Waiting until the last moment for a slow rolling ball, allowing the opponent to get to the ball and tip it away from the goalkeeper. Always go to the ball.

4.   Ball played with flat palms instead of the finger tips allowing for the creation of re-bounds. There must be "give" in the hands.

Illustration 18.

For extra safety, as soon as the goalkeeper makes contact with the ball, he can fall forward over the ball with his body, preventing re-bounds.

In each technique, the palms are pointed forward with fingers spread and the pinkies are turned toward each other, slightly touching to insure that the hands are behind the ball.

2.   Ground balls which are played to the side of the keeper must be worked on as follows:

A.   The goalkeeper takes several side steps, getting behind the ball, so that the ball is coming exactly straight at him (see Illust. 19).

Common Faults:

1.   The goalkeeper does not step quickly enough and the ball is still at the side of the body when contact is made. It is now possible for the ball to skip through the hands as there is not back-up cover (the body must be behind the ball in all catching where the weak "pinkie" fingers are inside — fingers pointing down). Get behind the ball quickly — speed is important for goalkeepers.

Illustration 19.
When stepping to the goalkeeper's left, it is the right knee which bends and the lower leg is held parallel to the goal-line giving balance. When stepping right, the left knee bends.

2.   Going further than the ball, being forced to play the ball behind your body.

In the run to the left side the right knee is down. In the run to the right, the left knee is down (see Illust. 19).

Common Faults:
1.   The wrong knee is placed on the ground. The proper technique is best practiced without the ball until the correct manner is comfortable and becomes natural.
2.   Placing the knee too firmly on the ground, makes the goalkeeper static as he can no longer maneuver if the ball takes a bad hop, changes direction or rebounds.
3.   Not getting behind the ball so that the body can act as back-up.
4.   The opening between the bent leg and the heel of the other foot is too big and the ball can get through.
5.   The upper body is not bent over the ball. If the body is straight and the ball suddenly jumps up then the rebound may go over the goalkeeper or bounce far away off his chest. But if the body is bent forward, the ball stands a better chance of staying in the area of the goalkeeper.

Drills:
1.   Play balls to the keeper - from about 6 yards out, softly and directly at him.
2.   Similar balls, but now the goalkeeper comes forward to scoop up the ball on the "run."
3.   Increase speed of ball - goalkeeper comes forward to scoop up the ball on the "run."
4.   Play balls to the left and the right of the goalkeeper from approximately 12 yards out:
      a.   goalkeeper quickly gets behind the ball;
      b.   goalkeeper picks up the ball on the run.

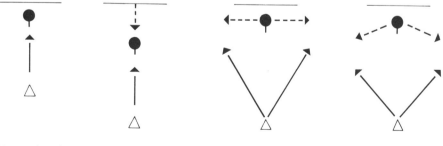

Illustration 20   Illustration 21   Illustration 22   Illustration 23

5.   Left and right side balls, but now goalkeeper takes diagonal run at the ball getting behind the ball, but in a more forward position from the goal.

6.   Same as above, but increase speed.

7.   Play the ball at the goal, but do not inform the goalkeeper where it is to be played. Vary the shots. The keeper must react.

Other possibilities:

a.   vary speed;

b.   vary spin;

c.   vary distance and position from which the balls are served.

It is the task of the goalkeeper to scoop up the ball as quickly as possible in a technically correct manner.

8.   Variables with several balls:

a.   played on the ground;

b.   vary the speed;

c.   vary the distance;

d.   vary the spin;

e.   vary the time between each ball.

NOTE: 1.   Besides serving as exercises to improve the goalkeeper's technique, conditioning can also be the objective.

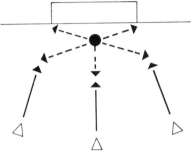

Illustration 24.

2.   By increasing the number of repetitions in a time frame, the goalkeeper will also make adjustments in his positional play.

4.1.3.2.Getting Out of the Way of Incoming Opponents

A.   Running at the ball in full sprint, scooping up the ball stepping to left or right, depending upon the opponent. Stepoff the left leg when going left and vice versa (see Illust. 25).

B.   Picking the ball up on full run and then forward diving to the right or the left. Notice take-off foot. Ball is completely covered on the ground. This driving technique must be practiced at first from a kneeling and then from a static standing position. Finally, it may be done over obstacles and to either side when the ball is coming in from the side. The ball is cradled at the chest and is not put in the area of the stomach which could cause injury. Caution: A long sleeve shirt and gloves with wrist protectors are recommended for the practice of this technique (see Illust. 26).

C.   Finally, as a last resort, getting out of the way by stepping to the side with a judo type roll, when nothing else is possible — this practice is dangerous and should be practiced before ever attempted in a game (see Illust. 27).

Common Faults:

1.   Stepping away with the wrong leg;

2.   Stepping out of the way too quickly, thus mishandling the ball, possibly leaving it right there;

Illustration 25. The opponent is coming to the left of the goalkeeper and he steps to the right.

Illustration 26. Forward dive to the left with the attacking player coming from the right.

3. Stepping into the opponent — the wrong decision. These two above techniques (Illustrations) should be practiced at slow speed with minimum resistance from the opponent at first, then gradually building up so that the goalkeeper can "read" the actions of the oncoming forward without error.

Illustration 27. The judo roll to step out of the way of the oncoming player.

Drills:

1. The ball is passed under an outstretched rope approximately 18″ off the ground. The goalkeeper picks up the ball on the run and:

a. steps sideways around the rope or over the rope, maintaining his balance;

b. pushes off with two legs and forward dives over the rope;

c. judo roll over the rope — first practice the judo roll without the rope or ball, then with ball only, then with rope only and finally with ball over the rope.

Make sure the above exercises are practiced to the left and the right.

2.   The goalkeeper must also practice these steps with the ball rolling away from him and this can be accomplished by passing the ball to the goalkeeper and then he intentionally mishandles the ball, pushing it several yards forward or to either side to sprint after the ball and pick it up on the run, avoiding the oncoming player or coach.

4.1.4. The Underhand Catching of Low Balls (between ankle and hip) and the Receiving of Balls at Stomach and Chest Height
While the ball often comes straight at the goalkeeper, the goalkeeper must also be ready to perform these skills after taking several steps to either side to get into the path of the ball.
   A.   Catching balls between ankle and hip height.
   B.   Receiving balls at stomach height.
   C.   Receiving balls at chest height.
In reference to the ball, in "A," above, the goalkeeper stands with legs slightly spread apart and holding an easy flexible stance. Do not lock the legs. The insides of the hands are pointing out (forward). Pinkies are pointing to each other and the hands make soft contact with the ball bringing it to the stomach area (see Illust. 28).

Illustration 28. Underhand catching of balls between ankle and hip height.

Common Faults:
    1.   Spreading the legs too wide.
    2.   Upper body too straight - arms and hands have difficulty meeting the ball - the body must be able to lean forward over the ball.
    3.   Legs are locked and are not flexible.
    4.   Hands on the side of the ball and not behind it.
    5.   Use of palms instead of finger tips giving unnecessary rebounds.
    6.   Body not square to the ball, an attempt to catch sideways - full body must always be between the goal and the ball.

Catching the Ball at Stomach Height

The catching techniques here are much like those for catching of the ball at ankle-hip height. The goalkeeper caresses the ball into the stomach area, however, rather than letting it slam off the stomach. There are often two sounds; the first sound of the hands making contact with the ball and the second of the ball being brought into the stomach area. As soon as contact is made, the arms and hands lock around the ball and the upper body bends forward over the ball (see Illust. 29).

Common Faults:
    1.   Legs are locked; if the ball should change direction the goalkeeper is caught in a static (frozen) position.

Illustration 29. Catching the ball at stomach height.

Illustration 30. Jumping to receive the ball at stomach height.

2.   The upper body is not bent over the ball - allowing for the possibility of a rebound back onto the field of play.

3.   The hands and arms close too late around the ball, allowing it to rebound back onto the field.

4.   Placing one hand above and one hand below the ball forcing the ball up and out.

The goalkeeper may be faced with three other maneuvers:

1.   Taking the ball at chest height with underhand positioning. . .the chest bone is hard and does not offer the soft cushion of the stomach. Hard shots should not be handled this way. . .the goalkeeper should catch overhand with the stong thumbs behind the ball, or if this is not possible, fist the ball out to safety.

2.   The goalkeeper may jump up to raise his body in order that the chest high ball is received at stomach height (see Illust. 30).

3.   With good timing the goalkeeper should reach the arms out to meet the ball, especially when there is an opponent near the ball (see jumping style used in Illust. 31).

Common Faults:
1. See B. 1, 2, 3, 4.
2. See six common faults of catching stomach height balls.

Drills:
To improve the goalkeeper's underhand catching ability at various heights:
A. Rapid fire shots at various heights from 8 yards out.
B. Changing speed of the ball.
C. Changing the distance, intermitenly from a far 11 to 20 yards to a close 5 to 11 yards.
D. Playing bouncing (skipping) balls right in front of the goalkeeper (especially with wet and very hard dry fields).
E. Forcing the goalkeeper to move sideways to play these balls (see Illust. 32a).

Illustration 31. Jumping to catch a chest high ball at stomach height.

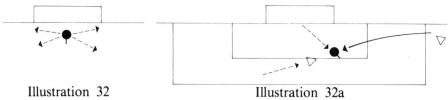

| Illustration 32 | Illustration 32a |

Example:

1.   The trainer serves the ball from the goal-line to a player standing at the edge of the goal area. The goalkeeper must run forward and/ or sideways to play the ball.

2.   The action (resistance - effort) of the attacker is increased (see Illust. 32a).

F.   Serving the ball from several positions; in front, at the side, to the left and right of the goal.

G.   Balls served in rapid repetition of each other until technique breaks down.

4.1.5. Overhand Catching

A.   Catching the ball at head height.

B.   Catching the ball at reach height.

C.   Catching the ball at jump height - highest possible height for the goalkeeper.

It must be realized that if the ball is not coming straight at the goalkeeper, he must move quickly sideways to accomplish getting his body behind the ball.

The fingers are formed in the shape of a "W" or fan, with thumbs and index fingers pointing at each other. The ball must be caught softly. The arms reach toward the ball, contact is made with the fingers, not the palms and the arms brought in (give) to cushion the flight of the ball. When contact is made with the ball the hands then close around the ball and the ball is brought to the chest or stomach (see Illust. 33 and 34).

Often there is a tendency to slap the ball down at the feet. This should be discouraged. It is a technique from the history of soccer before the ball was waterproofed and before modern goalkeeping gloves. The unwaterproofed ball was heavy and it was too risky to catch, therefore, the heavy shot was slapped down to stick in the mud. This must now be avoided, as it is no longer an appropriate technique.

Common Faults:

1.   Not using the fingers but the palms giving a slapping sound and a rebound. Use the fingers as in Illust. 33.

Illustration 33

Position of the hands for overhand catching.

Illustration 34. Catching balls at head height.

Illustration 35. Catching balls at reach height.

2.   Ball caught incorrectly with hands too far in the back or too much to the side (as in basketball) forcing a dropped ball.

3.   Wrists are bent too far back and the ball goes over the top of the hands and head into the goal.

4.   Arms are bent too early or too late - therefore providing less give - not taking the speed out of the ball.

Drills:

1.   Practice catching stomach, chest, and head high balls while in a kneeling position (develops soft hands and good give).

2.   Practice drop-kicking between two goalkeepers at short range to provide more power to shots, increasing speed and decreasing distance.

Catching Balls at Jump Height

Defending direct shots at goal and catching indirect attacks at the goal in the form of crosses.

The principle is the same as catching at reach height, however, the ball should be held in the outstretched position for one second when catching in "traffic" in front of the goal so as to not bring it down onto the head of a jumping teammate or opponent (see Illust. 36, stationary jump without pressure of an opponent).

A.   The take-off for the jump should be one legged, with the big thigh muscle of the opposite lifting leg giving power to the jump and protecting the goalkeeper against the on-rushing opponent. Footwork and timing is important and the goalkeeper must have the ability to jump off either leg, so that the leg nearest the opponent is not planted when contact with the opponent is made.

The goalkeeper will need practice in "judging" the ball so as to time the jump to make contact with the ball at the top of the jump and so as not to overrun the ball or run under it as is the fault of many young goalkeepers. When the goalkeeper incorrectly reads the flight of the ball and has to leap backwards to catch, he must often use a two footed take-off as in Illust. 36 and expose himself to injury in traffic as he has no protection. The goalkeeper must know in advance his:

-    path to the ball;
-    placement of his take-off foot;
-    flight;
-    place to make contact (catch) with the ball;
-    landing spot and method.

B.   Use the support of both arms (no one hand catching) for increased elevation of the jump.

C.   Running players with momentum can often jump higher with their heads than the goalkeeper from a stationary position. The ball must be caught at its highest point for the goalkeeper.

D.   The take-off leg is the landing leg.

With crosses, the goalkeeper is not dealing with direct shots, but indirect attacks at goal. . .he is not protecting the goal from a shot, but instead protecting the area in front of the goal (see Illust. 37).

Illustration 36. Directly defending the goal - catching balls at jump height.

Illustration 37. Indirectly defending the goal - catching a cross.

The training for direct and indirect defending of the goal by means of catching the ball at jump height is similar in nature.

Common Faults:
1.   Two footed take-off - the goalkeeper is extremely vulnerable here.
2.   Taking off on left leg and landing on right leg, will prevent the goalkeeper from having proper "hanging time" and force him more quickly to the ground, especially if the leg is active in other than prescribed technique.
3.   Using the leg to support the jump.
A.   Attempting to jump without use of the big thigh muscle for power and lift.
B.   Knee not sharply pointed forward, in direction of jump.

Illustration 38. Overhead catching, intercepting the cross (notice vertical jump of field player who had running start).

When the knee is not pointed forward enough the goalkeeper loses support (power) for his jump and his protection against oncoming players.

4. The ball not caught at its highest point (re-read section on timing).

5. The last step is too small and the goalkeeper does not go straight up, but forward at an angle thus losing height.

6. See numbers 1, 2, 3, 4, of A and B.

Drills:

Balls are given at jump height (lob and high bounces):

1. on the goal;
2. in front of the goal.

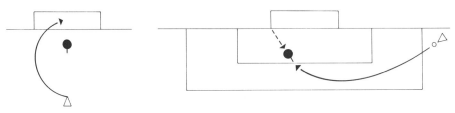

Illustration 39   Illustration 40

a. Ball is given at reach (jump) height for the goalkeeper to deal with from a standing position (see Illust. 39).

b. Running with two steps.

c. Running with several steps.

d. Increase speed of ball, from slow or fast.

e. Lobs, straight balls, spinning balls.

f. Increase the distance, 16 to 30 yards, now the goalkeeper has more time to view the situation, but judgement problems now become more severe (timing again).

g. Smaller distances 16 to 18 yards.

h. Positions in front of and to the side of the goal should be changed (see Illust. 41).

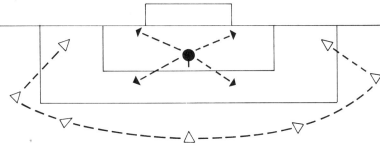

Illustration 41

i. Working in groups of three with opposition.

Trainer throws or kicks the ball above the head of the player and the goalkeeper climbs above this player to get the ball.

Illustration 42

The activity of the resisting player should be at first passive, then at 50%, then active - 75 to 90%, then finally under complete game conditions.

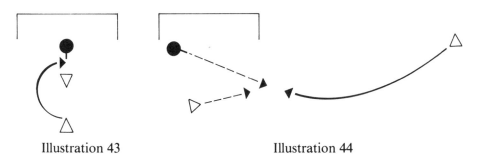

Illustration 43   Illustration 44

The goalkeeper starts at first with a stationary position in front of the goal (see Illust. 43).

Then the goalkeeper must run to the front of the goal to play the ball. Finally, the number of players should be increased.

4.1.6 Tipping the Ball Above the Crossbar
  a. Jumping up and tipping the ball over the bar backward.
  b. The ball is tipped over the bar by running backward and sideways.

Tipping should only be attempted as a last resort, when the goalkeeper has no chance to bring the ball under control. It is an emergency situation, and is mostly needed when the goalkeeper has been off his line for angle play and the shooter attempts to lob the ball over him, or when a power shot is deflected and is now spinning toward the crossbar. The goalkeeper should never calculate that the ball is going to hit the crossbar and he would be at a disadvantage if it were to do so.

Illustration 45. Tipping the ball over the bar with falling.

Rather than let the ball hit the crossbar, it must be tipped over the bar. Also, tipping must be done with care and execution so that a tipped ball does not hit the crossbar.

For practice the coach provides short services at the crossbar. Very quickly the goalkeeper must run and sidestep backwards while always facing the ball. There are two methods:
1. with falling (diving);
2. without falling.

If the ball is played too far behind the goalkeeper, he shall have to dive backward to make a last ditch effort to keep the ball out of goal. As far as diving (falling) after the goalkeeper has tipped the ball over the bar, he will need to turn in the air (kinesthetic sense) so that he is now facing the ground in order to absorb the shock of his fall (not land on his back) with his hands, arms and then the rest of his body (see Illust. 45).

Illustration 46. Tipping without falling.

The last backward step should use the outside leg to lift the body, the big thigh muscle providing the lift. After contact with the ball the body should be flexible in landing.

It is not always necessary to have to dive backward to tip the ball over the crossbar. A straight jump up may be all that is needed (see Illust. 46).

On a slow ball at the crossbar there are two possibilities for the goalkeeper.

1.   The wrist becomes flexible and turned in to lift the ball over the bar or;

2.   the ball is boxed over the bar. Boxing a slow ball at the crossbar can be risky because of the smaller surface of the gloved fist at the bar and the possibility of the ball slipping off that surface into the goal or even a complete miss.

Conclusion:

A.   The stretched open hand with the larger surface is safer at the crossbar.

B.   The lob must be boxed with closed fist if the goalkeeper is away from the crossbar, but under the bar the open hand may be used. . .keep in mind that the ball is always tipped by the hand closest to the ball.

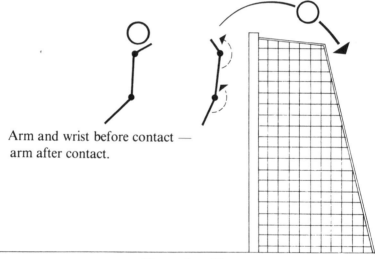

Arm and wrist before contact —
arm after contact.

Illustration 47

C.   It will take good footwork to run backwards and still face the ball... turning to side stepping action in order to place one hand closest to the ball.

If the run back to the goal is to the goalkeeper's left, the right hand must be used to tip the ball over the bar, and vice versa.

Common Faults:

1.   When running backward toward the ball, the keeper takes his eyes off the ball and turns his back toward the ball.

58

2. The ball, instead of being pushed over the bar, is played back onto the field.

3. On a slowly played ball, the ball does not get enough lift.

4. The backside of the hand faces the ball with the palm to the bar and the ball is played against the bar or into the goal.

5. Not using the closest hand to the ball.

Drills:

A. Goalkeeper throws the ball with two hands up high and tips it behind him, turns around and catches.

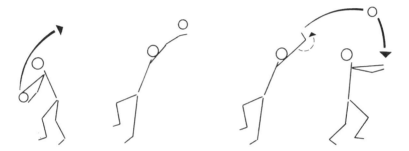

Illustration 48

B. Same as above, but with jump, take-off with both legs and goalkeeper reaches the ball at its highest point.

C. Throw the ball backwards at an angle, run backwards, tip the ball and catch it.

D. Same as above, but with a jump.

E. Trainer serves the ball and the goalkeeper tips the ball over the bar.

F. Trainer serves a lob.

G. Goalkeeper stands 3 yards from the goal. Trainer serves a straight ball whereby the goalkeeper runs quickly backward and tips the ball over the bar.

Illustration 49   Illustration 49a

H.   Same as G, but with a lob (see Illust. 49a)
I.   Increase the distance of the goalkeeper from the goal.
J.   Serving to the left and right of the goalkeeper.
K.   Serving from an angle forcing the goalkeeper to turn to go backward.
(see Illust. 50).
L.   Serving by means of kicking full volley or half volley kicks.
M.   Several players serving from several positions (see Illust. 51).

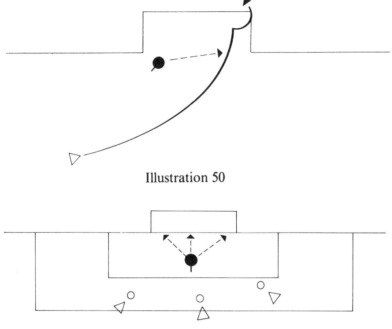

Illustration 50

Illustration 51

4.1.7. Boxing
A.   With two fists
B.   With one fist
I.   Boxing forward from the front of the goal
II.   From the sides

General Observation:
Boxing with two fists is the safest. The contact area is larger and also there is more strength with two fists rather than one. Distance is an important quality of a boxed ball. In certain situations the ball must be played with one fist (such as when the goalkeeper is caught in traffic or when the ball is coming from the side and the goalkeeper must keep its direction to play it over the heads of the opponents. There is a longer reach with one fist, but the loss of playing surface and power make this a risky play which, however, the goalkeeper must perfect to attain the next level of play.

Techniques:

A. Boxing with two fists:
    — curl hands to create a fist;

    — the thumbs are at the top and back, but not inside the fist;

    — the knuckles touch, but there is no pressure of one fist against the other as this would decrease the playing surface;

    — as soon as the flight of the ball is judged, the goalkeeper establishes his rhythm in attacking the ball;

    — the fists are brought to the chest;

    — the body is in a bent position;

    — just before contact with ball, the body explodes forward straightening the elbows;

    — contact with the ball is made just below the center axis and the arms continue their follow-through until completely straight. (The fists must be tight and wrists locked.)

Illustration 53. Boxing with two fists from a standing position.

Illustration 54. Boxing with two fists on the run and jump.

Illustration 55. Boxing with two fists while jumping under the pressure of opponents in traffic.

B. Boxing with one fist:
— close the fist tight so thumb comes to lie on top of the second knuckle;
— can be performed from a standing position or on the run;
— can be performed with one or more steps depending upon the flight of the ball and the path of the goalkeeper to play the ball at the highest point;
— body is bent, fist comes up to the chest and with explosive movement the arm is straightened thru the ball;

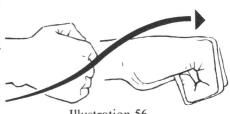

Illustration 56

— the fist is turned just before contact with the ball so the backside of the hand is facing upwards;
— the ball is hit just below the center point and the arm follows through the contact. (With timing, the ball may be boxed on the run, with a jump, with a running jump and in full flight. Timing must coordinate the several steps, the planting of the foot for take-off, the flight, the boxing of the ball and the landing position.
(see description as in catching a high ball).

Common Faults in A & B:
1. The body does not get poised (set).
2. Fists are not brought up to the chest.

Illustration 57. Boxing with one fist from a standing position.

Illustration 58. Boxing with one fist on the run — taking off with the planted leg — boxing in flight and landing on the original planted leg.

    3.   Making contact too early or too late — missing the full power of the explosion of the body into the ball.

    4.   Missing the underneath of the center of the ball, causing it to either go too high, straight up or directly down into traffic.

    5.   The ball is boxed back directly to the player or area of players from which it was crossed.

6. Faults with two fists:
    a.   both fists do not come evenly together to form one flat surface — this must be practiced;
    b.   not making proper contact with the ball, for example hitting the ball with the underside of the wrist or fists.
7. Faults with one fist:
    a.   ball hit with incorrect fist surface as in 6.b. above;
    b.   ball is hit with the wrong fist — a ball coming from the right should be hit with the right handed fist, for example, into the opposite direction and as far as possible (height and distance). It should be noted that hitting the ball with the "wrong" hand is better than no contact at all, however.

Drills:
Boxing with two fists:
    a.   From a kneeling (to get height) or a standing position, box the ball with two fists out of the trainer's hands to another player or into the goal (accuracy - see Illust. 59).
    b.   Increase the distance.
    c.   The trainer serves the ball to the goalkeeper and from a sitting position, then kneeling with follow-thru to finally a standing position the ball is boxed back to the trainer with accuracy.
    d.   Same as above with timed jump.
    e.   Trainer serves the ball up to the goalkeeper and he boxes the ball back to the trainer (see Illust. 60).

Illustration 59   Illustration 60

    f.   Same as above except with timed run and jump.
    g.   Trainer serves the ball from the back of the goal (behind) over the crossbar and the goalkeeper boxes for power into the goal (see Illust. 61).
    h.   Same as above except with run and jump.
    i.   From a service from the front of the goal the goalkeeper boxes the ball to one of the sides (see Illust. 62).

j.   Balls are served from the sides and the goalkeeper boxes the ball to the opposite side. With and without jump (see Illust. 63).

k.   Provide the placement of one or two opponents — repeat "Exercise j," and increase the involvement of the players from passive to active.

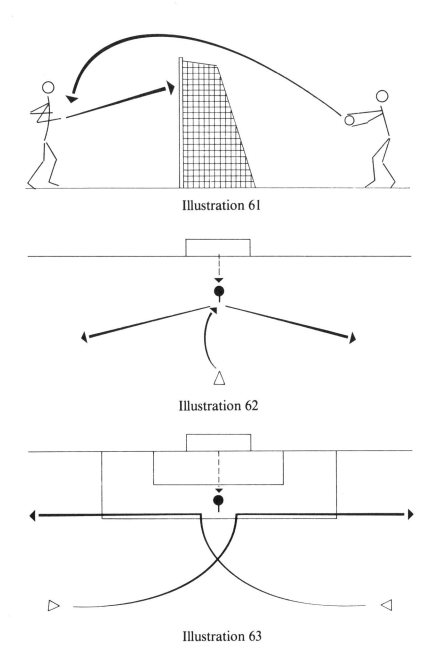

Illustration 61

Illustration 62

Illustration 63

I.   Boxing Balls Served to the Direct Front of the Goal

a.   Practice punching the ball with one fist out of the opposite hand, either into the goal (see Illust. 64) with power and accuracy or back to the coach.

b.   More poised boxing position, standing with left leg forward when boxing with the right hand and vice versa. Tense the body and box the ball away.

c.   Same as "b." above, only the goalkeeper throws the ball up high (see Illust. 65).

d.   The coach serves the ball and from a standing position the goalkeeper fists the ball using alternating right and left hands.

e.   Same as "d.", except with run and jump.

f.   Balls are served from three positions to the direct front of the goal, the goalkeeper comes out and with one or more steps, times a jump and boxes the ball to the sides (see Illust. 66).

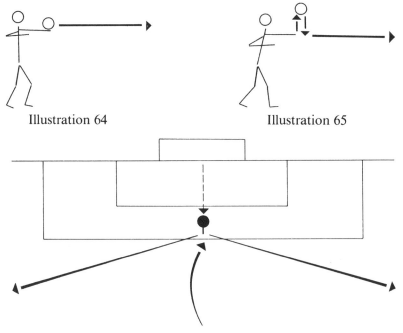

Illustration 64   Illustration 65

Illustration 66

g.   Repeat with several opponents.

h.   Increase the resistance of the opponents from passive to fully active.

II.   One Fisted Boxing from the Sides:

a.   Standing sideways, the goalkeeper boxes the ball out of his hand working toward the goal or back to the trainer (see Illust. 67).

b.   Ball is served up with the left hand and boxed with the right and vice versa (see Illust. 68).

c.   Throwing the ball up higher and boxing with the right hand so that there is a follow-thru with the right leg and vice versa.

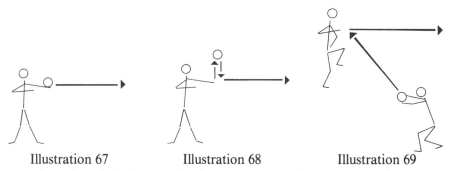

| Illustration 67 | Illustration 68 | Illustration 69 |

d.   Toss the ball up and (using an example of a ball boxed with the right hand from the right side) bend the right knee, point the knee in front of the body and turn the knee in the direction where it will be boxed. The trunk of the body remains in the original position (see Illust. 69). This exercise must be practiced from both the right and the left. The bringing up and pointing of the knee creates a tension in the body which can be transfered into the ball resulting in a powerful box of the ball.

e.   Ball tossed by the trainer, keeper boxes the ball with the quarter turn into a goal or to another player (see Illust. 69). Remember to turn the knee to the inside to create that necessary tension.

f.   Same as above with run of one or more steps, get set and then box the ball over the goal with height and distance to a target (accuracy).

Illustration 70. Boxing with one fist.
Note: Vertical Jump of Goalkeeper and Opponent.

g. Same as "e," but with a half turn.

h. Same as "f," but with a half turn.

i. Serving the ball with the feet from the sides (also with throwing).

j. With one or more opponents.

k. Increased resistance from passive to full competition.

Boxing with one or two fists:

a. At chest height the goalkeeper has a choice and should practice accordingly. Legs are wide spread making a strong, balanced stance. Box with two fists.

b. Now box with one fist, making sure the left leg is in front when boxing with the right hand and vice versa.

c. Now repeat above, but alternate choice after several repetitions.

d. At head height, repeat "a," "b," and "c" above with maximum jump.

e. At reach height, repeat "a," "b," and "c" above with maximum jump.

f. Sideways boxing with one fist in above exercises.

Boxing in other situations:

In other game situations, such as when a shot is taken from very close range or if the ball is extremely slippery, boxing may be employed. Boxing is often the safest method to handle the ball and the goalkeeper must be ready and have quick reactions to box the ball sideways away from the goal to decrease the possibility of a goal chance coming on a rebound.

Common Faults:

1. The ball is struck too low beneath the center and it does not travel a great enough distance away from the goal, but rather travels up in a lob.

2. The ball is struck too high above the center and goes immediately down, loosing speed in its flight away from the goal and especially on a muddy field getting caught without traveling a great distance.

3. Ball contact is made too early and not enough power is put into the contact, reducing distance.

4. The ball makes contact with the inside or side of the fist. Remember, however, that a save is a save and that this type of save is an emergency maneuver. Make the save. Watch out for the rebound.

Additional factors:

1. The chance of injury due to hyper-extension of the elbow in increased.

2. The change of a dangerous rebound is increased.

It is always better to tip the ball to the side of the goal or around the post. An open hand is longer than a closed fist, but not as strong. Strength must come with the jump and upper body extension, if using the open hand to get more of the hand onto the ball.

Illustration 71. Boxing the ball away in an emergency.

Drills: (See also: Building up, Falling, Diving and Flying.)

A. Trainer stands next to the goalkeeper approximately 1½ yards away with the ball in his hand. Goalkeeper pushes off from a standing position and boxes the ball with one or two fists out of the hand of the trainer.

Illustration 72

B. The ball is held by the trainer at heights that are varying between hip and the head.

C. The distance of the goalkeeper and the trainer is increased to the point where the keeper has to take one or more steps sideways to do this exercise.

D. Trainer stands now in front of the keeper and throws the ball, first only left and then only right. Thereafter, either way.

NOTE: Exercises "A," "B," and "C" may also be done with the trainer standing in front of the goalkeeper.

E. The ball is served strongly from a short distance near to the goalkeeper. He boxes the shot with one or two fists around the goal or towards the far sideline (reaction-fist-save).

Actions of the Goalkeeper:
1. from standing position;
2. with one step sideways.
3. with several steps sideways.
F. Playing to the goalkeeper from various directions (see Illust. 73).
G. Playing balls more rapidly after each other.

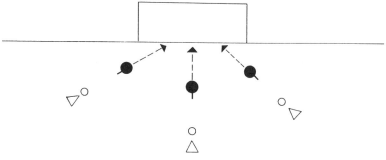

Illustration 73

NOTE: This exercise is also tremendous for the improvement of reaction time and conditioning. Training should be done towards the left, as well as, the right of the goalkeeper. A last situation where the ball may also need to be boxed is the lob, which because of lack of speed cannot be tipped, but has to be boxed away. There is too little strength in the hand for tipping, as the goalkeeper may be too far away from the bar to get the ball over by means of an open hand.

Drills:

A. The trainer throws the ball with a lob. The goalkeeper stands approximately 5 yards in front of the goal, then takes several steps backward and boxes the ball over the bar (see Illust.74).

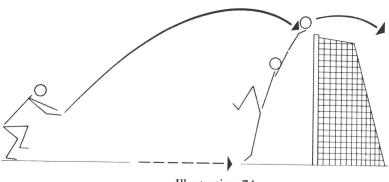

Illustration 74

B.   Similar distance between goalkeeper and trainer. However, the goalkeeper is further away from the crossbar, needing faster and more steps to get back.

C.   Serving balls more to the left and more to the right of the goalkeeper.

D.   Serving is replaced by kicking of volleys.

E.   The speed of the ball is increased.

F.   Several different directions (see Illust. 75).

G.   Increasing the frequency of services.

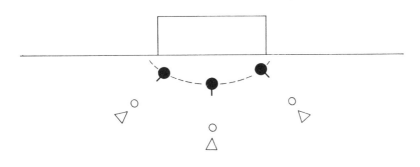

Illustration 75

NOTE: This is a tremendous series of exercises for the improvement of conditioning and the coordination of the left and right sides of the goalkeeper.

Illustation 76. Boxing to save a low shot from close range.

4.1.8. Falling, Diving, Flying and Saving in the Air

4.1.8.1. Drills - Falling Sideways

A. In a sitting position, balls are tossed to the goalkeeper, he catches and rolls over onto the side of his body. While rolling over it is important that one leg remains still and that the other forms a sharp point with the knee in the direction of the roll. When rolling to the right, the right knee remains still. The left leg is bent into a point and the body turns over (see Illust. 77).

Variations:
I. Catching balls to the side of the body.
II. Catching balls as close as possible near the feet. Thus, angled forward.

B. Catching balls from a kneeling position. The goalkeeper catches and rolls to the side of the body such as in *A* above (see Illust. 78).

Variations:
I. Catching balls next to the body.
II. Catching balls diagonally in front of the body.

C. Squating on one foot and on one knee (see Illust. 79).
1. Balls are tossed to the side at which the foot is on the ground.

Illustration 77. Falling sideways from a sitting position.

Illustration 78. Falling sideways from a kneeling position.

Illustration 79. Falling sideways from one foot and one knee (diving).

Illustration 80. Diving sideways from one foot and one knee (using the ball to break the fall).

Variations:
    I.   Catching a ball next to the body.
    II.   Catching balls diagonally in front of the body.
    III. Catching balls further away from the goalkeeper so that he must come diving out (see Illust. 80).

    2.   From the side where the knee is on the ground, the ball must be fed so that it arrives at the goalkeeper a maximum of 20 inches above the ground (this also is an excellent lead-up exercise for diving).

Variations:
    I.   Catching balls next to the body.
    II.   Catching balls diagonally in front of the body.
    III. Catching balls thrown further away from the goalkeeper.

    D.   From a squat position, the goalkeeper catches served balls and rolls as in *A* above (see Illust. 81).

Variations:
    I.   Catching ball next to the body.
    II.   Catching balls diagonally in front of the body.

    E.   Same as *D* above, but with take-off and actual flight (see Illust. 82).

Illustration 81. Falling sideways from a squat position.

Illustration 82. Diving sideways from a squat position (again note using the ball to break the fall).

NOTE: Balls should be played to the goalkeeper at several heights, from bowling along the ground to the height that is just catchable by the goalkeeper.

F.   From a standing position, head up and facing the ball. Balls are served near to the body. The goalkeeper catches the ball and rolls over on his side. The lower leg makes first contact with the ground, then the side of the body, and then the side of the shoulders. From this height it is not necessary for the goalkeeper to break his fall by using the ball to make first contact with the ground. Instead, from this lower height, the goalkeeper can close his hands around the ball and during the fall, bring the ball to the safety of the chest area (see Illust. 83).

Illustration 83. Falling sideways from a standing position.

Illustration 84. Diving sideways from a standing position with the ball close to the body.

G. Same as *F* above with less of a fall and more of a take-off into a dive. Landing on the side of the body (see Illust. 84).

H. Exercises *G* and *F* are repeated, but the take-off and dive must be over an obstacle, such as a stretched piece of rope or player on his hands and knees. Avoid using dangerous obstacles such as a team bench or track and field hurdle, as it unnecessarily puts added stress on the goalkeeper and further tests his courage.

I. Exercises *G* and *F* are done in graduated steps. First without the use of the ball, so that the goalkeeper can build-up his courage by breaking the fall with his hands. Next the ball can be boxed away; then a tennis ball can be caught and held. Finally, the proper catching of a full-size soccer ball with proper landing; bringing the ball to the chest and protecting the ball where appropriate.

J. Balls given at one height.

K. Increase the number of balls and frequency of services.

L. Balls at various heights, speed and frequency which will force the goalkeeper to:

 I. Catch and bring the ball to the chest.

 II. Protect the ball to the maximum (see Illust. 84).

 III. Box the ball away with one fist.

 IV. Box or tip the ball around the posts with two fists.

NOTE: All drills must be practiced to the left and the right, at first informing the goalkeeper of the direction. Upon accomplishment, the goalkeeper is now ready to perform the above drills without prior information from the coach as to the direction of the serve and the coach may alternate the direction as appropriate.

4.1.8.2. Progression of Sideways Falling and Diving Skills

Diving for low shots often finds the goalkeeper either too high above the ground, or too low, arriving late as he is held up by friction with the ground. The standing goalkeeper must lower his center of gravity and step in the direction of the dive to achieve distance and proper height. This is practiced by the serving of low ground balls into the corner of the goal and eventually raising the service to a maximum height of 30 inches.

A. See drills for falling sideways *A* to *D*. The goalkeeper must get low to the ground and as quickly as possible. With a step in the direction of the dive there is an explosion of power to the ball, but also coordinated and smooth contact with the ground, gliding along the surface.

Illustration 85. Diving for a low ball in reach of both hands and protecting the ball to the maximum.

79

Illustration 86. Diving for a low ball in reach of one (lower) hand and tipping or shoveling past the post.

Illustration 87. Diving (flying) to tip the ball past the post. Note: Flexibility of arched back enhancing flight.

With power take-off:

B.   Balls served further in the corner of the goal coming at higher speed may require the goalkeeper to dive, rather than step and fall to save. It is important to practice both.

1.   Catching and securing the ball after such a dive (see Illust. 85).

2.   Tipping the ball around the post after such a dive (see Illust. 86).

NOTE: The technique of diving under a 30 inch rope and gliding or sliding along the ground on the side of the body, the hips and even the open extended arm (without fear of injury as there is no height to the fall) must be practiced. In fact, on grassy or damp fields the sensation is indeed pleasurable. But on hard and dry fields, the traveling distance of the goalkeeper will be restricted and greater distance may have to be made with footwork and flight.

C.   Increase the speed of the shot, forcing the ball to be boxed away.

D.   Serve from several directions.

E.   Serves at high frequency (*A, B, C, D* - see Illust. 88).

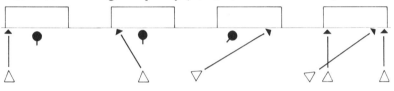

Illustration 88

4.1.8.3. Progression of Sideways Flying (Diving)

From the starting position, one or more sideways steps must be taken to build momentum (footwork). The body then turns inward toward the place where the ball is going to be at the catching or fisting point. The last step is a spread step which brings the goalkeeper face to face with the ball. With the big thigh muscle being used for power and the knee of the outside leg pointing to the upper corner, the goalkeeper can achieve a flight ranging from 2 to 7 feet.

A.   Build up the progression with the same drills for sideways falling as in *A* to *C* above.

B.   Serve balls in such a manner that the goalkeeper has to take one or more steps sideways (important footwork).

C.   Serve balls which force a spread step which turns the body inward and sideways.

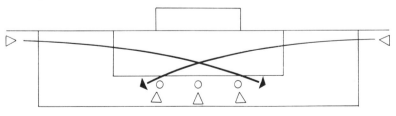

Illustration 89

Illustration 90. Taking one step and diving up sideways. Note the use of the ball to break the fall from this height.

D.   Serve balls from different areas to the side of the goal, causing the goalkeeper to do some indirect defending of the goal dealing with crosses. These are difficult saves and require courage for the goalkeeper in match situations, especially if the services arrive at a height lower than the heads of the opponents (see Illust. 89).

E.   Increase both velocity and frequency of services.

F.   Vary the services without rhythm or manner.

1.   The goalkeeper must make the decision to box the ball with one or two fists.

2.   Tip or shovel the ball around the post.

3.   Catch the ball in mid-flight, fall properly and secure the ball to the maximum.

Illustration 91. Footwork to gain momentum for a flying catch some 6 feet above the ground. Note the catching position of the hands, sight lines to the ball, steady head and using the ball to break the fall. Flight covered more than half the goal and the keeper's lands well past the post.

Illustration 92. Flying — note full extension of the body. Is it a save or a goal?

4.1.8.4. Flying to Tip the Ball over the Crossbar or Around the Upper Post

Technique:

The importance of footwork is becoming increasingly more evident to serious goalkeepers. Study Illustrations 90, 91 and 93 to check footwork.

It is the upper hand which touches the ball over the bar or around the upper post. The goalkeeper must parrallel his body to the ground to establish the upper hand. When going to the goalkeeper's left (Illust. 93) it is the right hand which is higher and must be used. Vice versa when going to the right.

Drills:

A.   Build up flying sideways just as in *A* and *C* above. Then induce the need to tip the ball over the bar as described on pages 84-85. Initially the coach or trainer serves balls from directly in front of the ball so that saves as pictured in Illustration 93 are demanded.

B.   Server now serves from the side. . .both left and right (see Illust. 94).

Common Faults:

1.   Take-off. . .footwork, step, knee and hip are not extended to the limit, hense the dive falls short and the goalkeeper does not reach the ball.

2.   The concentration on the dive is so great that the goalkeeper's hands do not get behind the ball properly and the ball is deflected into the goal. The dive can be perfect, but fail to save the ball. It is wrong to concentrate solely on style or what the goalkeeper looks like. . .the save is what counts.

3.   The palm of the hands plays the ball back on to the field, giving a dangerous rebound. . .the fingers must deflect the ball around or over the bar.

4.   Tipping errors (see these sections). Also do not try to catch a slippery ball at this height. There is not enough strength in the outstretched hands.

5.   Landing on the stomach. Extremely dangerous from great heights - use the ball to break the fall or practice rolling after tipping to absorb the shock. With low shots, stomach landing can allow the ball to roll under the body.

Illustration 93. Flying up to the height of the crossbar to tip the ball over the top. Note the footwork and large powerful step, plus breaking the fall with the hands and arms, then a shoulder roll.

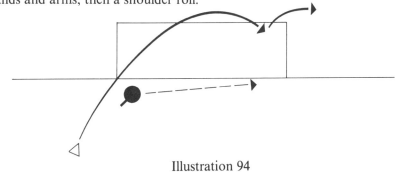

Illustration 94

6. The body remains too stiff, causing a landing of enormous impact instead of flexible rolling. . .increased chance of injury.

NOTE: The shock of landing is absorbed significantly by the goalkeeper who is able to roll several times around the length of his body after saving. . .especially low balls, but avoid such rolling while holding the ball unless an absolutely sure grip is present.

4.1.9. Diving Forward

Balls that bounce in front of the goalkeeper often cannot be caught against the chest while standing tall, and should be caught and protected with a forward dive.

Technique:

With low balls the goalkeeper must place his hands under the ball and then cover the ball with his body over the top of the ball to keep it from bouncing out and rolling away. The goalkeeper's fall is broken by the back of the hands, forearms, elbows and knees.

If the ball comes in higher, then the goalkeeper has three other possibilities:

A. Diving forward and getting the ball before it bounces.

B. Placing the hands on the top of the ball and trapping it on the short hop, not letting it bounce, then bringing it under the chest.

C. Boxing the ball with one or two fists, especially in traffic when the risk of a dropped ball becoming a dangerous goal chance is high. The movement is similar to a volleyball player diving forward to save, and breaking the fall with his hands and upper body in a smooth gymnastic maneuver.

Common Faults:

1. Goalkeeper dives forward too high and the ball goes under the body.

2. In case *B*, the hands get to the ball too late and it bounces up and over the prone goalkeeper.

3. Boxing errors (see boxing with one and two fists).

4. Catching errors (see overhand and underhand catching).

Drills:

1. Four balls in a square, approximately 2½ yards apart. . .distance depends upon size, skill and power of the jump of the goalkeeper. . .forward diving to each ball using overhand topping of ball (see Illust. 95).

2. Goalkeeper rolls ball in front of himself and dives forward to secure ball while it is rolling away (see Illust. 96).

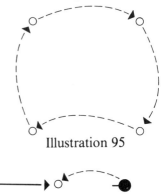

Illustration 95

Illustration 96   Illustration 97

3.   The coach serves the ball along the ground and the goalkeeper charges the ball and dives forward to trap the ball against the ground (see Illust. 97).

4.   Arching balls are served and the ball is caught with a forward dive before it hits the ground (see Illust. 98).

5.   Same as above, except goalkeeper catches the ball just after it bounces.

6.   Variations of *4* and *5* above.

7.   The coach serves a straight ball to the goalkeeper who dives forward and boxes the ball back onto the field. . .review the build up of proper boxing techniques (see Illust. 99).

8.   The coach serves the ball by means of drop-kick or full volley at the goalkeeper from varied distances, arch and speed. The goalkeeper decides which of the above techniques to use.

Illustration 98. Forward diving, catching the ball before it bounces.

Illustration 99. Forward diving boxing the ball away with two fists. (Keep eyes on ball after contact).

4.1.10. Backward Diving

Normally when the word diving is used we think about diving forward or sideways in relationship to the ball and the feet. In some situations, however, the goalkeeper must execute a backward dive as in the following:

1.   A shot against the post or crossbar whereby the ball bounces back and the only way to save would be with a backward dive.

2.   An opponent dribbles past the goalkeeper or knocks the ball around and past the goalkeeper in a breakaway situation and the goalkeeper must dive backward to make a play.

Technique:

From the standard take-off position. . .the ball is kept in sight. . .the head turns around in the direction of the ball and after that the trunk and legs turn.

Variations:

A.   From the standard take-off position the goalkeeper dives and makes a quarter (¼) or one half (½) turn in the air.

B.   From the standard take-off position the goalkeeper takes his one quarter or one half turn and then dives. . .this is more time consuming and is actually forward diving after a turn. The fall is broken with the front and side of the body.

Drills:

1.   The ball is placed behind the goalkeeper about 2 yards and he turns either right or left with a backward dive (see Illust. 100).

2.   The ball is rolled behind the goalkeeper from either side. The goalkeeper dives backward to save. . .work both sides (see Illust. 101).

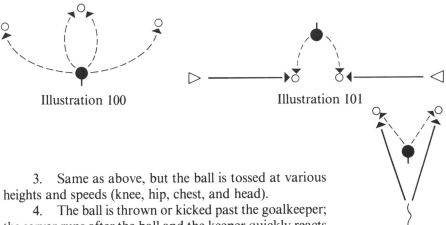

Illustration 100

Illustration 101

3.   Same as above, but the ball is tossed at various heights and speeds (knee, hip, chest, and head).

4.   The ball is thrown or kicked past the goalkeeper; the server runs after the ball and the keeper quickly reacts to dive backward and get the ball under pressure of the running player. . .left and right. (See Illust. 102)

Illustration 102

Illustration 103. Backward diving with a one half turn in mid-air.

4.1.11. Diving at the Feet of the Opponent

During the course of play, opportunities present themselves whereby the goalkeeper can best save a goal chance by diving at the feet of the opponent who has possession of the ball. The goalkeeper in doing so, attempts to get the ball before the opponent shoots, as he shoots, or just after the shot is taken. The size of the goal is reduced by the goalkeeper's presence and the pressure often forces a hurried shot.

The goalkeeper must occupy himself with an attempt at:

A.   Taking over the ball.

B.   Using proper techniques and body control to avoid a foul against the opponent and also concern himself with possible injury.

Illustration 104. Backward diving under pressure of opponent and time. Note position of hands to top of ball to bring it in.

The best technique for diving at the feet of the opponent includes the following: using the entire length of the body to block the path of the opponent; using the top arm with bent forearm at the leg of the opponent to somewhat protect the head of the goalkeeper; using the lower hand (underarm) to make contact with ball and pull the ball toward the body.

Common Faults:

1.   The goalkeeper's timing is incorrect and he throws himself too early or too late at the feet of the opponent. The timing is essential. Practice concept 2 (page 30), must be understood until the goalkeeper develops proper timing and is able to choose the exact moment to attack the man and the ball in this situation.

2.   The goalkeeper does not use the full length of his body and leaves a portion of the goal exposed.

3.   The goalkeeper does not place the upper part of the upper arm against the shin of the opponent and does not keep his head far enough away (see Illust. 105, notice position of head).

4.   The goalkeeper does not place his hands strongly enough at the ball and the field player wins the tackle, knocking the ball loose.

5.   If the goalkeeper does not get the ball before the shot or at the same time as the shot (goalkeeper's block tackle), then he must throw this full body at the shot to take the shot as in Illustration 106.

Drills:

1.   The coach stands still with a ball at his fcct. Thc goalkeeper comes out of the goal with hands down at sides (see Illust. 105), and proceeds to make a long barrier with his body parallelling himself along the ground to make contact with the ball as previously described above. Practice coming out both right and left.

2.   The coach dribbles the ball softly at a slow pace toward the goalkeeper. The goalkeeper times his run looking for the moment that the coach is not in complete possession of the ball and could pull it back or knock it away. Repeat above, right and left.

Illustration 105. Diving at the feet of the opponent.

3.   The coach dribbles at full speed in the direction of the goal and prepares to take a shot. . .the goalkeeper dives at the feet of the coach at the moment possession of the ball is lost in shot preparation. The goalkeeper must maintain a long barrier for a long period of time.

The practicing of the so-called *goalkeeper's block tackle,* whereby the goalkeeper makes contact with the ball with his hands at the moment of shot is very important and there are several drills:

1.   The goalkeeper lies on the ground with the ball in his hands, arms outstretched and the coach kicks at the ball with the goalkeeper tensing up for each kick to absorb the power of the kick.

2.   Place a ball between the goalkeeper laying on the ground and the standing coach. When the coach pulls back his leg to make contact with the ball, the goalkeeper attacks the ball and readies for contact.

3.   The coach dribbles the ball as in *3* above, but the goalkeeper parallels himself into the path of the coach and saves the ball at the same time it is kicked by the coach. . .a block tackle.

Illustration 106. Throwing the body to back a shot. Note long barrier.

4.1.12. Sliding into a Loose Ball at the Feet of the Opponent

On certain surfaces and under certain conditions, the goalkeeper may find it advantageous not to throw his body into a loose ball in front of the opponent, but rather to slide several yards along the ground and slide into the ball.

Techniques:
The basic techniques required for this save are the same as throwing the body as described above except the maneuver is performed earlier and at a further distance away from the opponent and the ball. Success is due to the smooth surface such as wet grass, astroturf or muddy goal area.

Common Faults:

Same as throwing the body at the feet as described previously. Also, technique cannot be performed on other than special conditions.

Drills:

NOTE: The chance of injury is high if these drills are practiced on anything but a wet surface field.

1. Ball is stationary. The goalkeeper takes a run of about five yards and approximately 2 yards from the ball, begins his slide toward the ball (see Illust. 107). NOTE: Instead of getting hands directly to the ball the goalkeeper can attack the ball with his upper body and stomach area.

2. Now the ball is played at the goalkeeper and the goalkeeper starts his run as soon as the ball is played. . .repeating *1* above.

3. Same as above, except ball is played to the right and left of goalkeeper (see Illust. 108).

4. The coach dribbles toward the goalkeeper and the goalkeeper begins his slide, making the goal smaller through angle play and pressure, and the coach tries to beat the goalkeeper by means of a firm shot which is cut off at the moment of shot by the sliding goalkeeper (see Illust. 109).

5. The coach plays the ball into the penalty area where the goalkeeper and the opponent duel for the ball — the goalkeeper sliding into the path of the ball at the feet of the opponent. (See Illust. 110).

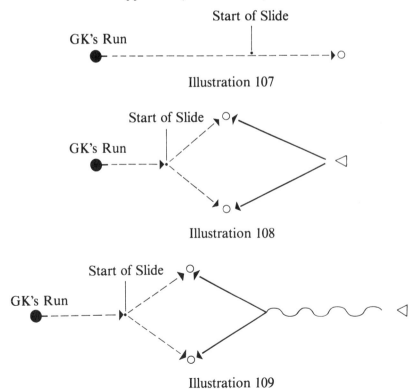

Start of Slide

GK's Run

Illustration 107

Start of Slide

GK's Run

Illustration 108

Start of Slide

GK's Run

Illustration 109

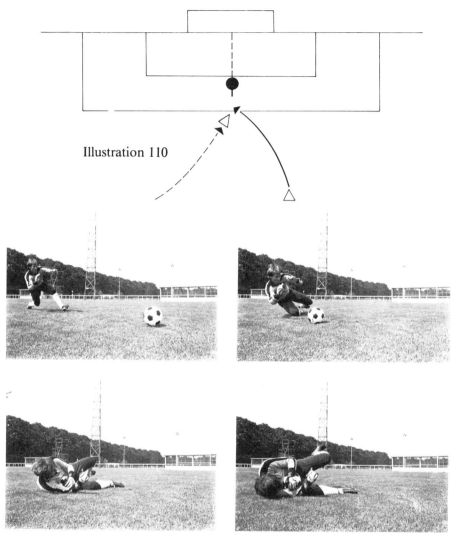

Illustration 110

Illustration 111. Sliding to the right to collect the ball before the opponent can get to it.

4.1.13. Playing the Ball Outside the Penalty Area

Modern soccer now finds the goalkeeper playing as sweeper for the sweeper, often having to make important plays outside of the penalty area to prevent the development of goal chances and also to make key plays as the last defender. In theory, the goalkeeper should play the ball as far from his own goal as possible.

But the goalkeeper with improved foot skills and field playing ability has many other opportunities available to him and if team possession of the ball can be maintained through his play outside of the penalty area, a terrific advantage is gained, otherwise the ball should be played to the side or touch line and even over the goal line for a corner-kick, because the goal is deserted and the risk is high.

94

Illustration 112. Throwing the body to save at the feet of the opponent. Note position of the forearm between head and opponent's foot.

4.1.13.1. Playing the Ball with the Feet

If there are no opponents in the area than the goalkeeper can:

A.   Dribble the ball with ease back into the penalty area and play it out in a normal fashion.

B.   Play the ball to a teammate. . .but exercise extreme care as the goal is empty. . .if opponents are near, safety first is mandatory, play the ball for distance.

Common Faults:

1.   Indecision by the goalkeeper. . .once a decision has been made to leave the goal, do so quickly, decisively and continue the play. . .do not stop and get caught half way out of the goal or going backward after stopping.

Drills:

1.   Goalkeeper positions himself at the 12 yard spot. The coach plays the ball through in such a way so as the goalkeeper must leave the penalty area to play the ball before the on rushing opponent (see Illust. 113).
2.   Same as above, but a bending service (see Illust. 113).
3.   Same as above, but bouncing pass (see Illust. 113).

2. Same as above, but a bending service (see Illust. 113).
3. Same as above, but bouncing pass (see Illust. 113).

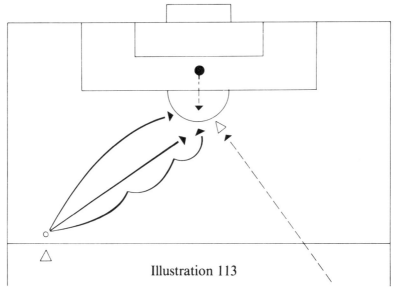

Illustration 113

4.1.13.2. Playing the Ball with the Head

Indentical to the requirements of 4.1.13.1., except the ball should be headed as far as possible.

Drills:
Same as above (see Illust. 113), except balls are played in at head height with straight, lob, and high bouncing services.

4.1.13.3. Tackling

The techniques of slide and block tackling must be mastered by the goalkeeper. When the risk of losing a block tackle is 50/50 or greater, the goalkeeper must make an important decision. . .whether or not to take a possible caution and direct free kick by playing the ball with his hands outside of the penalty area. . .after all. . .such direct kick is less dangerous than having the goal scored. When the ball cannot be played by means of foot or head than the hands are a last resort.

4.1.14. Emergency Defending

Every goalkeeper has witnessed the following situation: the keeper dives to the right and the ball is slightly deflected by a defender and now changes direction. In an emergency, the goalkeeper makes a miracle foot save going the other way. This is only one example, there are many and they are difficult to train for, as these are reaction saves and require somewhat unorthodox movement.

Some possible drills include the placement of a large number of foreign objects in front of the goal, such as traffic cones, coaching bags, medicine balls and corner flags or coaching sticks and have the goalkeeper stay on the line behind these obstacles to play shots taken by the coach and/or teammates along the ground which deflect off the obstacles at the last second and changes direction in front of the goalkeeper.

4.1.15. Reaction Drills

Objective: To sharpen and maintain the reaction time and reflex action of the goalkeeper.

NOTE: While the goalkeeper does not often have to save by means of his reaction to some noise or other sound stimulus there are a series of drills which utilize the reaction to sound as this does help sharpen reaction conditioning.

Drills:
1.   The coach and the goalkeeper stand face to face, approximately 2-5 feet apart.
A.   The coach holds the ball above his head and then drops the ball. . .the goalkeeper reacts and catches the ball before it hits the ground (see Illust. 114).
B.   Same as above, except the coach holds and drops the ball from varying heights, depending upon the reaction of the goalkeeper.
C.   Same as above, except the goalkeeper clasps his hands behind his body, then folded in back of the body, folded arms in front of chest, hands on head, arms outstretched above the head.
2.   Goalkeeper has his back to the trainer.
A.   The same variations as with *1* above, except the coach gives a verbal command as to when the goalkeeper should turn and to which direction (left to right) to catch the ball before it hits the ground (see Illust. 115).

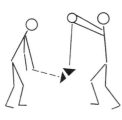

Illustration 114

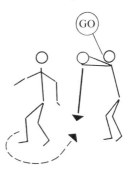

Illustration 115

NOTE: The coach should drop the ball rather than throw it to the ground.

    3.   The coach and goalkeeper are facing each other approximately 5 yards apart.
    A.   The goalkeeper places his hands at his side next to his body and the coach throws the ball or punches the ball toward the area of the goalkeeper's face. . .the goalkeeper reacts and catches the ball in front of his face.
    B.   The goalkeeper clasps his hands behind the back.
    C.   The goalkeeper folds his arms behind the back.
    D.   The coach serves the ball harder.
    E.   The coach shortens the distance between himself and the goalkeeper.
    F.   The rhythm of the services is changed.
    4.   The goalkeeper stands with his back toward the coach at an approximate distance of about 6 yards.
    A.   The coach serves the ball at the area of the head of the goalkeeper. . .then the coach gives the signals to turn. . .the goalkeeper turns his head and then catches the ball.
    B.   Same as above, except the signal is given later.
    C.   The coach kicks the ball and the goalkeeper reacts to the sound of the foot striking the ball.
    D.   The distance is shortened.
    E.   The balls are shot harder.
    5.   Use of the kick-board or bang-board (see Illust. 116 - portable goals brought to the stationary kick-board make for realistic drills).
    A.   The coach serves a ground shot to kick-board.
    B.   The coach serves by means of a drop-kick.
    C.   The coach serves by means of a volley-kick.
    D.   Decrease the distance.
    E.   Faster shots (harder).
    F.   Increase frequency of shots.
    6.   The distance of the coach and the kick-board approximates 7 yards, but the goalkeeper is approximately 3 yards from the wall (see Illust. 118).
    A.   The coach kicks the ball off the ground.
    B.   The coach drop-kicks.
    C.   The coach volley-kicks.
    D.   Harder shots are kicked off the board.

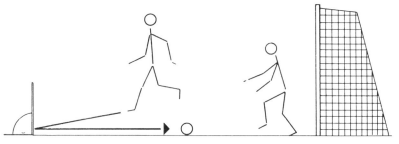

Illustration 116

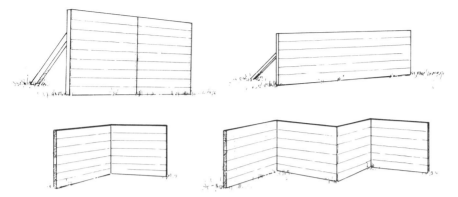

Illustration 117. Various kick boards which can be used in goalkeeper training.

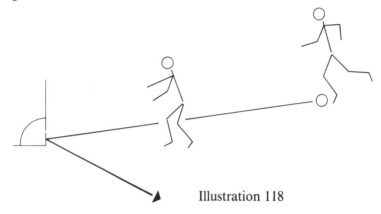

Illustration 118

E.   Increase the frequency of shots.

F.   Change rhythm of delivery of shots.

The difference between these two groups of drills is that in the first group the coach is within view of the goalkeeper while in the second (see Illust. 118) the coach is behind the goalkeeper and the keeper must react to the sounds of delivery.

7.   The distance between the goal and kick-board is now 8 yards (see Illust. 119).

A.   The goalkeeper kicks the ball from the ground against the board.

B.   The goalkeeper kicks the ball by means of a drop-kick.

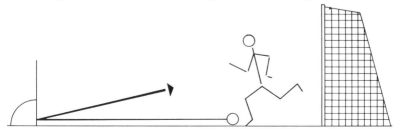

Illustration 119

C. The goalkeeper kicks with full volley.

D. The goalkeeper kicks with greater force.

E. Decrease the distance.

8. The goalkeeper and coach face each other approximately 7 yards apart. The goalkeeper serves the ball to the trainer who returns with a volley or drop-kick back within reach of the goalkeeper (see Illust. 120).

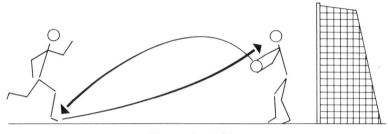

Illustration 120

4.2. The Attacking Skills of the Goalkeeper

4.2.1. Punting from the Hands

4.2.1.1. Volley

The ball is kicked directly from the air (see Illust. 121). Of great importance is the tossing or dropping of the ball, as it must be done with accurate precision. It is better to drop the ball from the hand opposite to that of the kicking foot to clear the way for a follow-through, although some goalkeepers are successful with a two-handed delivery.

In the back swing of the leg, the goalkeeper fully extends the instep of the foot, to the extent of pointing backward. The leg is also fully extended and follows-through after contact, as far as possible.

The position of the non-kicking foot and the twist of the body determines the trajectory of the ball after contact.

If the non-kicking foot is forward even to the point of being past the ball at point of contact then the trajectory will be low or flat. If the goalkeeper bends his body backward, then the ball will go up in the air, as it will if the non-kicking leg is well behind the ball at point of contact. The arms are held out for balance.

Advantage of a low, flat kick: The ball reaches a teammate quickly allowing for fast counter-attack.

Disadvantage of a low, flat kick: There is risk of an interception shortly after delivery.

Illustration 121. Volley-kick from the hands.

Advantage of a high kick: Distance without risk of quick interception.

Disadvantage of a high kick: The ball takes too long to get to the area of the goalkeeper's teammate, hense opponents have time to get into position as well.

Common Faults:
1. Incorrect toss — ball too forward or too close to the body, or too much to the left or right of the goalkeeper.
2. The back swing is too small, thus full power is not put into the ball, minimizing distance.
3. The ball is not kicked in the center and curves or slices off target.
4. The instep is not extended and locked minimizing strength at the point of contact with the ball, decreasing distance.
5. The kicking leg is not fully extended and again maximum distance is not reached.
6. The non-kicking foot is too far forward or back and the trajectory of the ball is either too high or too low.
7. The body is bent forward too far or too far back again, negatively influencing trajectory of the ball.
8. The arms are not active enough against the position of the legs (balance) and stability is lost, influencing the flight of the ball off target.

Drills:
1. The goalkeeper kicks the ball to the coach accurately at approximately 6 yards distance. The instep must be extended and locked (see Illust. 121a).
2. Same as above only balls are kicked with an arc or curvature to the hands of the coach.
3. Same as above restricting to flat or straight balls (see Illust. 122).
4. Same as 2 and 3 above, except increase the distance to 35 yards or more, depending upon physical dimensions of the goalkeeper.

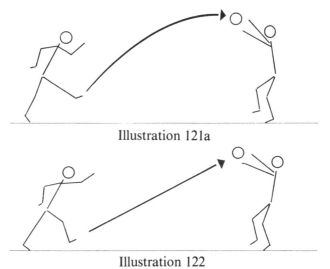

Illustration 121a

Illustration 122

5. For longer distances, goalkeeper takes a run of two - three steps.

6. The goalkeeper dribbles the ball to the edge of the penalty area and from there distributes by means of a volley-kick to one of three players who by way of their run demand the ball (see Illust. 123).

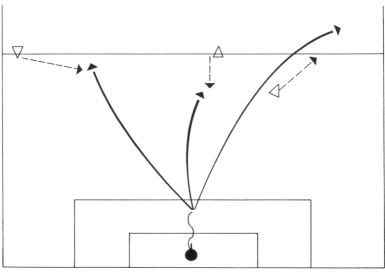

Illustration 123

The organization of this drill can also be in the following manner:

A. Two goalkeepers kick to each other (making sure proper no bounce catching above the head where possible takes place).

B.   The goalkeeper kicks to a target (goal - bench, tire) and a ball returner stands ready to return the ball quickly to maximize practice (several balls can be used).

Goalkeeper Games:

7.   Two goals approximately 30 yards apart (junior players closer). Two goalkeepers and one ball. Accurate full volleys to score against the opponent. The ball must be kicked from where it is caught. Corner kicks give the ball back to the shooter to start again from the goal line. Rebounds across the mid-field line are forfeited. Emphasis on catching and holding, and of course, obvious kicking proficiency (see Illust. 124).

8.   Two goalkeepers, one trainer and 10 balls. The trainer chips or shoots the ball to the first goalkeeper who catches the ball and tries to score on the other goalkeeper by means of a volley-kick. Change keepers and sides of service (see Illust. 125).

Illustration 124

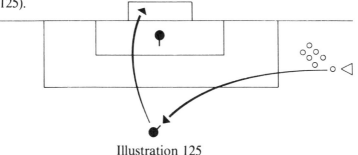

Illustration 125

4.2.1.2.   Drop-kick

The drop-kick is performed by bouncing the ball in front of the body toward the side of the kicking foot and immediately kicking the ball on the short hop. The dropping of the ball must be accurate and perfect if the kick is to be similarly accurate. The toss of the ball can be by means of two hands (more control) or by one hand (opposite to that of the kicking foot for best results).

The distance of the back swing of the kicking leg depends upon the time allowed by the toss, the more time the greater the swing and therefore, the more power put into the kick, hense greater distance. The kicking foot must be locked and extended downward with toes pointing downward or even backward. After the ball is struck, the leg continues to follow through in the direction of the kick.

The non-kicking leg is placed to the side of the ball and the trajectory of flight of the ball depends once again on whether the player leans backward and to what degree. The further back the lean, the more height to the kick. Once again the arms play an important role in body balance (see Illust. 126).

Illustration 126. Drop kick.

Drills:

1. The same drills that are used to practice the volley-kick can be repeated for the drop-kick, except of course, that the ball must be kicked on the short hop or bounce.

Advantage to the drop-kick: The ball can be hit on a straight trajectory directly to a teammate and the ball can be easily controlled and more importantly shielded from the opponent, making the accurate drop-kick very difficult to intercept.

Disadvantage of the drop-kick: The margin of error is greater; the ball will not bounce high enough on soft ground and will bounce erratically on uneven fields, reducing the chance for an accurate kick. In addition, a small error in the placement of the non-kicking foot greatly effects the trajectory. The ideal drop-kick has a low trajectory covering the field quickly and directly to its target.

Common Faults:

1. Same as with the volley-kick described above.
2. To kick the ground before the ball.

Reasons:

A. Shoes are too big.

B. Feet are too big — players with a small foot have less problems with the drop-kick as they are able to get their foot properly under the ball.

4.2.2. Distribution by Hand

4.2.2.1.Rolling (bowling)

The ball is bowled over a short distance, rolling along the ground to a teammate.

For a right handed player, the stepping motion (footwork) follows the sequence commonly used by bowlers (three-step) left-right-left-bowl. Of course, if the bowling distance is short (teammate close by) a single left footed step may be all that is necessary. It is important to hold the ball securely, bringing it back with two hands so as to not lose possession and then to swing the right arm forward with follow-through delivering a ball which does not bounce, but instead (as in bowling) rolls cleanly and smoothly along the ground (see Illust. 127).

NOTE: The goalkeeper must bend at the knees to present a synchronized fluent motion which will provide a service which does not bounce, but instead is easy for the teammate to receive.

Technique is vice versa for left handed servers.

Common Faults:
1. The serving hand leaves the ball too late or too early and the ball starts bouncing.
2. Knees do not bend, therefore, the ball is dropped rather than placed on the ground causing the ball to bounce.
3. The arm does not fully extend at the elbow and the ball is served too slowly.

Drills:
Other than actual practice of this simple exercise, there is no need to drill repeatedly. In normal practice situations the coach often asks the goalkeeper to deliver a ball to him and on these occasions the goalkeeper should deliver accordingly under the scrutiny of the coach who will correct errors and reinforce positive action.

4.2.2.2. Sling or Whipping Throw (sideways and overhand)

The ability to cover long distances by means of a throw is directly influenced by the spin on the ball which causes it to curve or slice away from the target and the trajectory necessary to cover the distance quickly.

To perform correctly the ball must be held in front of the body with the throwing hand with spread fingers behind the ball and the other hand placed in front of the ball as a guide. The stepping motion left-right-left for the right handed thrower is similar to that in bowling except that on the third step there is a strong definitive move forward and the entire body comes into play extending and following-through into the direction where the ball is thrown.

There are major differences between the sidearm and overhand sling or whipping throws.

Illustration 127. Distribution through bowling technique.

With the sidearm throw, the ball is brought back below shoulder height and then the arm is brought forward so that the ball leaves the hand at the side of the shoulder and also at that height (see Illust. 128). However, with the overhand throw the ball is brought back above the shoulder and thrown from there (see Illust. 129 - sometimes referred to as a baseball throw).

In either case the motion must be done quickly, but with rhythm. The ball should not have too much trajectory or spin and must be thrown as accurately as possible to avoid interception.

NOTE: To assist the teammate's reception of a thrown ball it may be thrown to the chest, thigh, head or foot. A bounce will take off some of the pace (speed) of the ball, helping a teammate's ability to receive the ball simultaneously increasing the chances of an interception. (Also, the effects of weather and surface conditions must be considered.)

Illustration 128. Sidearm sling technique.

Common Faults:
1.　The serving hand is not placed correctly behind the center of the ball, therefore, reducing the ability to put all the power behind the ball necessary for a long accurate throw.
2.　The ball is let go too soon or too late.

Disadvantages:
1.　The ball spins off going too far to the left or right.
2.　The ball gets too much of an arch and remains in the air too long enhancing interception or bounces too early; looses speed and also risks interception.

Illustration 129. Overhand (baseball throw) technique.

Drills:

1. Start to practice accurate throws which are easy to control (receive) with a distance of 10-12 yards between two goalkeepers or the coach and goalkeeper.

2. Increase the distance to 20 yards and practice the proper left-right-left stepping rhythm for the right handed thrower aiming the ball at the body of the other goalkeeper or coach.

3. Increase to maximum throwing distance with proper stepping rhythm to include throws which reach the target on a fly and also on a bounce, with major concentration on the ball's ability to be received by the target person with ease.

4. From the edge of the penalty area the goalkeeper throws balls out to moving teammates who best position themselves to receive a throw. The teammates vary position and direction of runs.

5. An excellent drill would have one defending player less providing zonal coverage of players trying to get free to receive the goalkeeper's pass.

Goalkeeper's Games:

6. Two goals approximately 20-30 yards apart as in Illust. 124 with each goalkeeper trying to score by means of a thrown ball played under similar rules as described earlier (page 103).

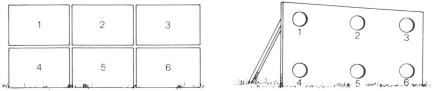

Illustration 130. Numbered goal and other possibilities for throwing.

4.2.2.3. Straight Throw

4.2.2.3.1. Overhand Straight Throw

The ball is brought back with two hands next to the shoulder at head height. The serving hand is directly behind the ball and the movement of delivery is similar to that of a shot putter. . .when standing the goalkeeper extends the elbow forward pushing the ball away. The goalkeeper can choose his steps accordingly to the direction he decides to deliver the ball, and since the stepping motion is not necessarily involved in the force behind the ball the goalkeeper can deceive the opponent by stepping one way and delivering the ball to the opposite direction (see Illust. 131).

Drills:
See drills for sidearm, overhand whipping throws.

4.2.2.3.2. Sidearm Straight-through Throw

The entire body must lean to the right for right handed throwers, so that the ball is thrown from a lower height thus reducing its ability to bounce up and providing a throw which stays low, yet covers ground quickly due to the force that the goalkeeper is able to get behind the ball (see Illust. 132). This throw is especially useful in indoor soccer as it is fast, accurate and covers tactically reasonable distances for that particular brand of soccer.

Common Faults:
Indentical to those involved in the other throws described previously.

Drills:
Same as above.

7. Throwing at the target goal, aiming for the posts or crossbar. . .two goalkeepers contest against each other for points.

8. Dividing a goal up into squares for target practice (see Illust. 130). The coach may call out a number at the last second so that the goalkeeper is forced to accurately alter his throws.

Illustration 131. Straight (shot-put) overhand throw.

4.2.3. The Goal-Kick

4.2.3.1 The Short Goal-Kick

A goal-kick whereby the goalkeeper places the ball just outside of the penalty area to a teammate in order to receive the ball back immediately, so that it may be punted out of hand or otherwise tactically employed to use time or alter the defending positions of the opposition; or to put a teammate into immediate attack.

The short goal-kick is usually taken very quickly, so as to not give the opposition time to set up to possibly catch one or more opponents out of the play (off the field, loss of concentration; back to goal). The kick must be accurate, is usually taken with the inside of the foot and the goalkeeper must immediately support (run after the pass), so that the distance is kept small in order that the teammate may pass the ball back to the goalkeeper safely (see Illust. 133).

110

Illustration 132. Straight sideways (indoor) throw.

4.2.3.2. Long Goal-kick

With the longer goal-kick the objective is still the same, to reach a teammate. With this in mind the goalkeeper can take considerable time to:

1. pick up the ball;
2. place the ball properly;
3. take a run.

He may do all of these in an attempt to:

A. Improve his concentration for the taking of the goal-kick.

B. Get a visual image of the playing field, the position of his teammates and opponents and decoy in whatever way possible to enhance that ball

Illustration 133. Short goal-kicking.

possession is maintained. Of course, the use of a lot of time has the disadvantage of permitting opponents the opportunity of picking up loose teammates. . .the goalkeeper must judge all of this in relation to the score and time remaining in the game.

111

The taking of a goal-kick has many important considerations, not the least of which is the placement of the ball. The ball should be placed on an elevation and definitely not in a hole. If the ball rolls off the elevation while the goalkeeper is taking his run, he should stop and replace the ball properly. Take no chances.

The taking of a good goal-kick requires proper technique for success, and is not a question of power. The non-kicking foot is placed slightly behind the ball. The trajectory of flight is determined by the placement of the non-kicking foot and the body position. When the ball must be kicked straight and low, than the non-kicking foot is placed closer to the ball or even with the ball. If a high trajectory is required the goalkeeper must place his foot further behind the ball, although by bending the body forward to some degree the ball can be kept lower. By bending the body back the ball will achieve height, and success has to do with the swing of the leg and the force of movement of the leg as it strikes the ball. Is the leg swinging-through up or is it still swinging down?

To get full power the goalkeeper must bring his kicking leg back as far as possible (the heal is at hip height). The ball has to be hit with the full instep (and the instep and ankle must be locked). In many cases the ball cannot be hit with the full instep pointed downward, therefore, the ball has to be hit with the full instep pointing sideways. . .this is why the approach to the ball is taken from the side in a quarter circle run (see Illust. 134).

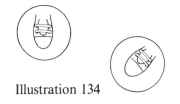

Illustration 134

Notice in Illustration 135, the use of the arms to keep balance and to serve as a counter-motion to the action of the legs. The leg swing has to be natural, flow evenly and not be interrupted.

Drills:
1. The distance of the coach and the goalkeeper is approximately 20 yards. . .they face each other. With technical accuracy the goalkeeper takes goal kicks in the direction of the chest of the coach or the goalkeeper can practice taking goal-kicks over the back of the goal, maintaining height and accuracy to the chest of the coach or other goalkeeper.
2. Increase the distance to the goalkeeper's maximum range.
3. The coach moves right or left — goalkeeper must provide proper goal-kick service on the run.
4. The coach signals for the ball to be delivered to chest, head, feet etc.

Illustration 135. Long goal-kicking .

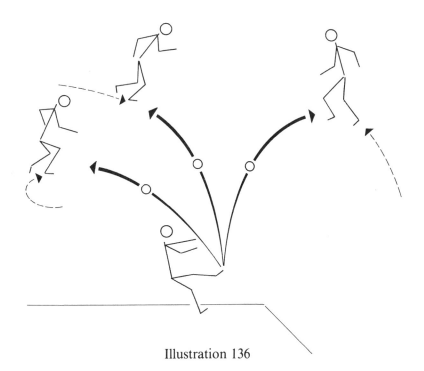

Illustration 136

Chapter Three

Tactics

1. Introduction

The goalkeeper's principle function is the prevention of opposition goals and the reduction of goal scoring chances. To accomplish this, the goalkeeper must practice the many diversified game situations which result in goals, and remember all of these to the point of eliminating all possible errors.

While most game situations have standard goalkeeping responses, there are many specific idiocyncracies of goalkeepers which are unorthodox solutions to the problems and if successful, these should not be discouraged.

The following factors need to be considered:
1. the size and condition of the goalkeeper;
2. weather and field conditions;
3. the style of the goalkeeper;
4. the goalkeeper's quickness and creativity.

2. Positioning and Angle Play
2.1. Various Game Situations
    A. Defending the immediate danger of the goal:

Game Situation: Shots taken at goal from several different directions and distances.

Answer: The goalkeeper rarely plays on the goal line, because by doing so the goal looms too large and inviting to the shooter. The goalkeeper should reduce the size of the goal and make himself bigger by coming off the line with proper angle play.

The near or short corner is most important and must be protected to the maximum. Goals should never be scored between the goalkeeper and near post. When the shooter is coming in from the side, angle play is easier as the goalkeeper has less to cover and the goal appears smaller.

The goalkeeper should visualize imaginary lines from the ball to each goalpost, which forms a triangle with the goal line (see Illust. 137). The goalkeeper divides the triangle in half, coming off the line to a comfortable position whereby the near post is maximumly covered and the far post can be saved with a minimum dive. Remember that angle play is three dimensional and that by coming out too far the goalkeeper will expose the top of the goal.

The goalkeeper can only come out to the point of his ability to return backward to the crossbar to save.

Illustration 137 diagrams the semi-circular path of the goalkeeper in front of the goal along which the goalkeeper positions himself to deal with various shots. At all times the goalkeeper must be able to get to the near post before the shot.

Of course, there is no near post when the shooter is coming down the middle, and the goalkeeper must come off his line to get as close as possible to the ball in a standing stationary position, ready for the shot, remembering of course, the top of the goal . . . the third dimension (see Illust. 138).

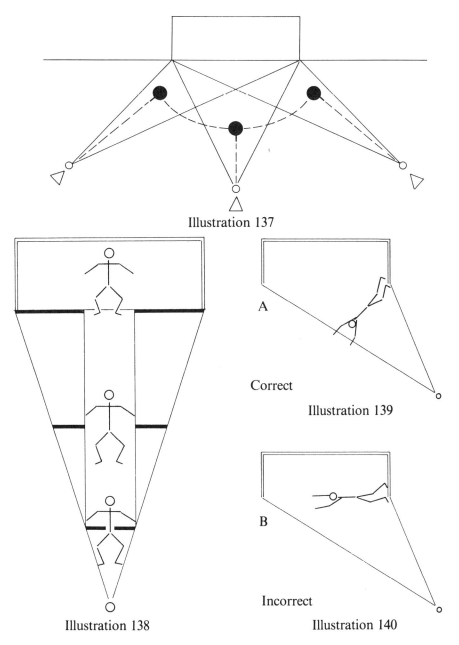

Illustration 137

A

Correct

Illustration 139

B

Incorrect

Illustration 138

Illustration 140

When diving to the short corner, the goalkeeper must be aware of his path and the danger of the post, always making sure that he dives in front of the post to avoid injuries. When diving to the far corner, the goalkeeper must plan on landing so that his hands could come on top of the ball, rather than the emergency of tipping it around the post or deflecting back onto the field (see Illust. 139). There should be no guess diving — everything has a purpose. The points of the shoes should always point at the direction of the dive where contact will be made with the ball. Illustration 140 is incorrect as opposed to the proper angle play in Illustration 139.

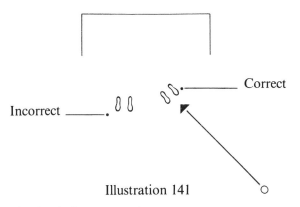

Incorrect _____. 𝟬 𝟬

Correct

Illustration 141

When angle play is faulty and dives do not cover the entire goal the coach must point out the position of the feet at the time of the dive, and these should always be directly pointing at the ball (see Illust. 141).

NOTE: In positioning himself with angle play, the goalkeeper must realize that the danger of a lob shot to the top of the goal is minimized by the extra time that a lob shot stays in the air, and the hopefully high quality of the goalkeeper's footwork will enable him to step sideways and backward to play the ball.

Game Situation: An opponent runs from mid-field alone on the goalkeeper, a typical lvl breakaway.

Answer: Through anticipation and reading the game the goalkeeper is already positioned in the area between the penalty spot and the edge of the penalty area. If the player passes the ball too far in front of him as is often the case, while running at top speed and being chased from behind but still having to look up to find the goal and goalkeeper, then the goalkeeper must immediately attack this situation and play the ball even if it is outside of the penalty area. If the opponent maintains good control, however, the goalkeeper must secure proper angle play and wait for the right moment. In any case the goalkeeper must not *sell* himself too early or come out without control as there is always the danger of a lob shot over his head. The goalkeeper cannot take a position so far out in relation to the ball and attacking players whereby he would be unable to get to the crossbar in the case of a lob shot.

Game Situation: When the defender needs to play the ball back to the goalkeeper, this should never be across the goal, but instead to the side of the goal.

Answer: The goalkeeper must demand the ball and point to the side of the goal whereby the pass should be made. Poor communication in this instance has often resulted in embarrassing self-goals (second fear of goalkeepers). The goalkeeper should not leave the angle of play until he is sure that the pass can be safely made to the side of the goal without error. This must be rehearsed over and over in practice. With confidence in his teammates, the keeper can anticipate the pass back, but must always be ready· to react quickly to make an emergency recovery in front of the goal.

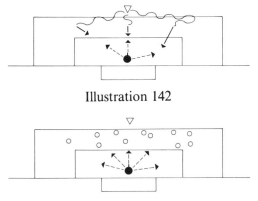

Illustration 142

Illustration 143

Drills:

1. Objective: To prepare for situations in front of the goal which need emergency reaction or change of direction (agility).

A. The coach or trainer dribbles left or right (vice-versa), fakes (feints), and then shoots with surprise (point of the toe; off foot ect.). The goalkeeper moves with him and reacts accordingly to save (see Illust. 142).

B. Eight to twelve balls are randomly placed around the penalty area. The coach kicks each ball randomly and the goalkeeper must save, react or get up (recover) to quickly save the next. Depending upon the ability of the goalkeeper, the coach can allow more time between shots. The coach may also follow-up on any rebounds (see Illust. 143).

NOTE: Balls that are saved should be tossed to the side of the goal.

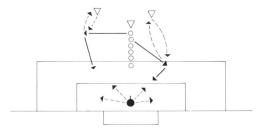

Illustration 144

NOTE: This drill can serve as a conditioner for the forward players who must run back quickly to ready for the next pass, as well as, serve as an aid to finishing. For extreme physical demand only one forward player is used, changing sides from which the shot is taken. The goalkeeper should be given at least enough time to be able to make a play on each shot. There is no practice shooting the ball into the empty net.

C. Two players line up on each side of the penalty area and the coach is between them with a number of soccer balls. The coach tips the ball wide and the running player shoots at goal (see Illust. 144).

D.   The coach stands between two players at the edge of the penalty area. The ball is played between the three and the goalkeeper adjusts his position accordingly. A player may be chosen ahead of time to shoot or this decision may be made independently. Rebounds should be followed-up (see Illust. 145).

E.   Four players form a square and play the ball around and through the square. Four corner flags or cones are placed within the square to form goals. The goalkeeper follows the ball, running from goal to goal around each pole (see Illust. 146). Shots at *goal* are randomly taken, the goalkeeper must adjust his angle. Drill can also be done with three players in a triangle, using three poles.

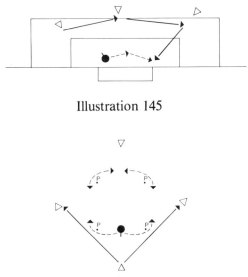

Illustration 145

Illustration 146

The following variations could be used:
1.   The ball is passed in a pre-established direction around the square.
2.   The ball is passed in a haphazzard uncertain direction.
3.   Ground or air balls only, forcing different kinds of shots.
4.   The shooting player changes positions in front of the goal forcing a change of angle.
5.   The coach may take a position in the square with two players; a player with a strong right foot is on his left and a player with a strong left foot on his right. The coach can lay-off the ball to either player for a changed angle of shot.

F.   The coach plays a soft pass in either direction along the edge of the penalty area. The player runs along the line and shoots to the short or long corner. The goalkeeper must adjust his position to best be able to save (see Illust. 147).

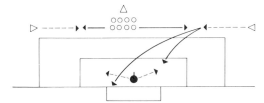

Illustration 147

2.1.1. Possibilities that Exist between the Goalkeeper and the Opponent with the Ball at his Feet

NOTE: The goalkeeper advances out of the goal or along the arch of angle play in front of the goal as long as the opponent does not have the ball on his foot. The goalkeeper must not be advancing or adjusting his position at the moment the shot is taken. There is always the very real danger that the shot is taken while the goalkeeper is adjusting his position and the keeper is caught standing on the wrong foot. Often great goals are scored just past the goalkeeper's foot which cannot be moved as it is supporting the total body weight. Great goal scorers are aware of this and these goals are not scored by chance. The goalkeeper must always be in the ready stance when the ball is being prepared to be shot.

Opponent	Shoots a hard straight shot from long distance.
Goalkeeper	Angle play should render the shot less difficult — catch and hold the shot — as last resort deflect the ball over the crossbar or around the post for a corner. No rebounds back onto the field.
Opponent	Lobs the ball over the goalkeeper's head.
Goalkeeper	Do not panic. The goalkeeper must realize that the ball will be in the air for a longer period of time and that he can without doubt cover the distance back to the post faster than the ball. He must use proper footwork, to accomplish this, however.
Opponent	Advances on the goalkeeper to several yards out and fires a hard, straight shot.
Goalkeeper	Decrease the angle as much as possible and hope for a quick reaction save.
Opponent	Attempts to pass the goalkeeper with the ball.
Goalkeeper	1. Look for a moment where there is not clear possession of the ball and attack the ball by diving at the feet of the opponent.
	2. Attempt to force the opponent to the side of the goal, decreasing the shooting angle and winning time (delaying the shot) so that a teammate may get behind the goalkeeper to save off the line should the shot beat the keeper. The opponent may hit the side of the net or be otherwise forced out of play. In any event, the goalkeeper must apply pressure.

119

Opponent   Plays the ball past the goalkeeper in an effort to catch up to it to knock it into the empty net (see Illust. 148).

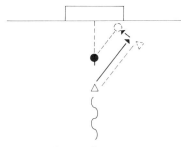

Illustration 148

Goalkeeper   The goalkeeper must turn, and quickly track down the ball, diving to get it before the opponent or placing his body between the opponent and the ball within playing distance, blocking his ability to shoot.

NOTE: The closer the goalkeeper gets to the ball, the more difficult it is for the opponent to score.

Game Situation: The attacker is running toward the goal with the ball, but a defender is running right with him.

Answer: This is one of the most difficult situations for the goalkeeper. The rule of thumb is that the goalkeeper never leaves his goal to interfere with a duel between an attacker and defender. The keeper should stay on his angle and give the defender a chance to make a play. This situation tests the cooperation and understanding between the defender and the goalkeeper like no other. It is evident that the longer the defender and goalkeeper play together and practice game situations together, the more likely good decisions will be made. Hense, the importance at minimizing substitution in the back. With proper understanding, the defender can set up the attacker and play him into the path of the goalkeeper . . . the two set a trap and the attacker runs into it. This takes time, patience, understanding and great tactical sense.

2.1.2. Defending the Immediate and Less Immediate Danger in Front of the Goal

Game Situation: The opponent is coming at the goal from the side, continues to the goal line and rolls the ball backward across the goal area (see Illust. 149).

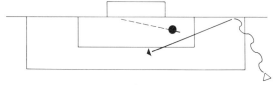

Illustration 149

Answer: If the opponent is running at full speed and he just gets to the line to keep the ball into play, then the cross (roll back) will be fast and hard. In this case, the goalkeeper should place himself in front of the goalpost and one yard out from the goalpost (see Illust. 149). If the opponent reaches the goal line at less than full speed, then he has more possibilities.

1.　He can shoot directly to the near post (see Illust. 150).

2.　He can cross the ball at about four yards in front of the goal (see Illust. 151).

3.　He can continue to the goal-line where he then will try to beat the goalkeeper across the goal with a hard straight cross (see Illust. 152).

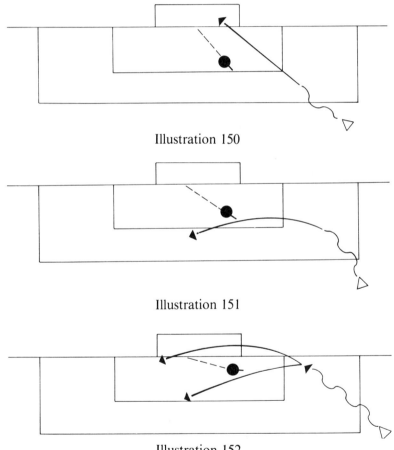

Illustration 150

Illustration 151

Illustration 152

The keeper must deal with each situation as it arises and understand each possibility. He should attempt a direct first-time interception. If the ball passes him, however, he must turn around and face the new situation.

Game Situation: The opponent is dribbling the ball along the touch line (side-line) and is plannning to cross the ball.

Answer: The goalkeeper can count on that from this situation, it is the usual intention that the player is trying to cross the ball, and the keeper can position himself for the cross. Remember, however, that there are miscues which will take a direction to the goal or the cross can be deflected in the direction of the goal.

There are two possibilities:

1.   The goalkeeper stands two and a half yards from the goal line and approximately one and a half yards from the back post. Because the ball is coming from a great distance, the goalkeeper has time to judge the curvature, trajectory, and runs of the opponents. The goalkeeper can cover large amounts of ground during the time the ball is in the air (providing he has good footwork -see Illust. 153).

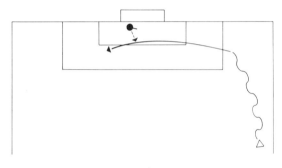

Illustration 153

2.   If the opponent gets to the goal line as in Illustration 154, the goalkeeper can position himself 3½ yards from the goal line and one yard from the back pole, as the opponent must pull the ball back away from the goal line out of fear of knocking it off the field or too close to the goalkeeper (see Illust. 154).

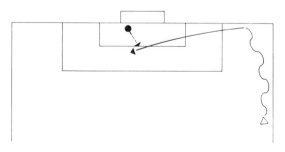

Illustration 154

NOTE: If the ball goes through all the incoming players and the goalkeeper as well, because he cannot intercept the ball (too hard—too high), then the goalkeeper must immediately position himself for the new situation.

Drills:

Objective: To improve play in front of the goal.

A.　Long crosses from the side of the field crossed from the goal line (approximately) (see Illust. 155):

　　a.　from a standing, stationary position;
　　b.　after a dribble.

Illustration 155

Variations:

1.　Balls are crossed to within five yards of the front of the goal. The ball is in flight a long time and this should not present a problem for the goalkeeper. The coach must demand that the goalkeeper execute all attempts at catching the balls technically correct.

2.　Increase the distance to between 5 to 18 yards, balls should be struck to the near and far post at different speeds.

3.　Variation of curve . . . inswinger, outswinger, straight or ground crosses.

4.　Placement of opponents under the following stages of activity:
　　a.　passive;
　　b.　half active;
　　c.　full activity;
　　d.　match situations.
Increase the number of opponents.

5.　Add defenders in match-up situations.

B.　Repeat *A* above, but alter the directions of the crosses, coming from all over the field as in game situations (see Illust. 156).

C.　After catching the cross the goalkeeper must immediately make an accurate distribution:

1.　by throwing to a player on the opposite side of the field from where the cross was made;

2.　to a teammate who gets open for a pass;

3.　kicking for distance and accuracy (a - drop-kick, b - volley) to a free mid-fielder.

D.　Short crosses taken from close to the edge of the penalty area.

NOTE: In dealing with crosses the goalkeeper does not always have to catch the ball . . . any satisfactory contact with the ball which causes even a slight variation in its course often in enough to throw the incoming players off, reducing their ability to head the ball accurately. Catching is best, boxing for height and distance is second best and a deflection is better than nothing. The goalkeeper must not allow a cross to go unchallenged. Short distance headers and volleys by opponents often result in goals because the goalkeeper is not set for the shot and the change of direction is too sudden. Goalkeepers must increase their range to deal with all crosses inside of the penalty spot and depending upon the height of the cross, inside of the penalty area.

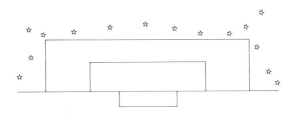

Illustration 156. Positions from which the ball may be played.

The goalkeeper must practice to increase his range and the coach should serve balls between the goal line and the penalty spot. An excellent teaching aid is the *Jugs Shooting Machine* (see Illust. 157), which can accurately serve balls consistently to the exact spot desired. Of course, Jugs can only serve a stationary ball, but it can serve inswingers, outswingers and straight crosses without unnecessary strain on the coach or field players which may occur with steady chipping or driving balls from the corner spot. The goalkeeper will need to work, therefore, on:

a. stationary balls - inswingers, outswingers and straight;
b. balls crossed after a dribble down the line;
c. balls shot across goal which are too high or too low;
d. reading the intent and possibilities of the opponent, timing the flight of the ball and fast footwork to weave through traffic accordingly.

Illustration 157

Drills:

a. The goalkeeper positions himself on the goal line at the center of the goal and takes a straight forward run to intercept the cross (stationary crosses).

b. Crosses taken after a dribble to the goal line, the goalkeeper reads the possibilities (speed and position of the opponent or coach) chooses his alternatives and advances accordingly to intercept the cross (see Illust. 158).

NOTE: The six yard box (goal area) belongs to the goalkeeper. Opponents shall not be permitted to receive a ball inside the goal area.

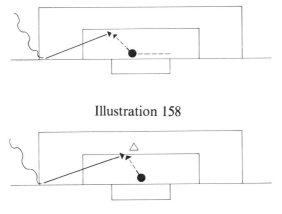

Illustration 158

Illustration 159

With the addition of one or more opponents, the practice session should continue within the following sequence regarding the behavior of opponents (see Illust. 159):

a.   passive;

b.   half-active (50%) - the opponent runs to the crossed ball forcing the goalkeeper to move quickly on a diagonal path to the highest point at which the ball can be caught before it is able to be played by the opponent;

c.   active;

d.   duel with complete opposition.

E.   Same as above with the following additional possibilities (see Illust. 160).

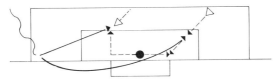

Illustration 160

The coach dribbles the ball to the goal line with two players making runs — the first to the near post and the second holding out the the far post. The coach crosses the ball:

1.   Only to the near post — the keeper must get to the ball before the opponent.

2.   Only with a lob to the far post - the goalkeeper attempts:

a.   to intercept the lob. If this does not succeed, the goalkeeper;

b.   quickly positions himself for the new situation and reacts accordingly (for head ball, full or half volley, roll back, whatever).

3.   The coach does not inform the goalkeeper, he must anticipate, read and react accordingly.

F.   Two players position themselves outside of the penalty area, ready to *sprint* to receive crossed balls from the coach (see Illust. 161). Notice direct path to the ball taken by player running to the near post and the bent run of the player hanging out at the far post. These runs must be tactically correct in order for the player to be positioned with proper timing to strike the ball at goal. The ball is crossed after a dribble down the line and the goalkeeper must deal with this crucial situation as there are two possibilities in addition to the speed and power created by the sprinting run.

The presence of this extra attacker makes rebounds and dropped balls very dangerous, the goalkeeper must make every effort to catch and hold the cross and otherwise play the situation if he is unsuccessful.

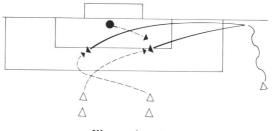

Illustration 161

2.2. Other Game Situations

2.2.1. Corner Kicks

There are differences of opinion regarding the philosophy of defensive corners, especially in regard to coverage at the back post.

There are those who believe that the back post is the goalkeeper's responsibility, and that a field player should not be wasted at the back post, as he will be needed more in front of the goal to duel with opponents in as much as a player is already assigned to the near post (mandatory). Others believe that a player at the back post provides extra security if the goalkeeper is unable to handle the corner under pressure and the back post defender can clear the ball off the line as a last resort, especially if the ball is played back into the goal area after a less than satisfactory clearance by a defender or goalkeeper on the corner kick. If two defensive players are used to cover the posts, the most courageous header must be at the near post, as this is where the most difficult contests for the ball will take place. Defensive corners must be practiced and there should never be goal allowed from a corner kick, it is a 100% goal situation without proper coverage and all of the team must be assigned a role to defend the corner. The opponents taking the corner have one player off the field, another in their own goal and probably one or more defenders hanging back to avoid a quick counter attack. If all defensive players are utilized and understand their roles, the defense shall out number the offense 11 to 7 or 11 to 8. If everyone does their job, there will be no danger.

FINAL NOTE: The goalkeeper must demand that the defenders at the goal posts take an active role and do not become ball watchers, holding on to the post. They should be positioned so as to be facing forward to see the entire field and the opponents, and they should pitch in toward the center of the goal if the corner kick allows them to do so. In this way they can assist the goalkeeper and touch a ball past the post for another corner in an emergency.

2.2.1.1.The Inswinger

The inswinging corner, curving toward the goal is extremely dangerous for the goalkeeper, especially when driven at head height across the goal, as it is difficult to intercept in front of the charging attacker at the near post. The goalkeeper must have the assistance of a player fronting the ball at the corner, 10 yards from the ball to force the corner to be played either out of bounds which is sometimes the case or played much higher over the fronting player giving the goalkeeper a chance for a play or further away from the near post, throwing off the run of the charging opponent, and his ability to take a dangerous header at the near post.

In addition a second defender must be placed about 6 yards away from the near post near the corner of the goal area to charge onto a driven inswinger and to prevent a clear run at the ball by the opposition. A triangle of three players (see Illust. 162) is formed by the player fronting the ball, the player at the near post and the player 6 yards out from the near post. This triangle helps minimize the threat of an inswinging corner driven to the near post. These positions are mandatory.

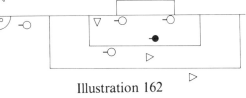

Illustration 162

2.2.1.2.   The Outswinger

The outswinging corner kick curving away from the goal is very difficult for the goalkeeper to judge . . . will it be in his range when it gets to his playable height and can he get there through the maze of players in front of the goal? Again a player must front the corner, to force the kicker to play the ball above him and provide that extra height and time for the goalkeeper. The goalkeeper should position himself well in front of the goal line to get a starting chance at the ball . . . and must realize the time that the ball will be in the air to make his play (see Illust. 163).

2.2.1.3.   Short Corners

With two of the opposition at the corner kick area, one defender ten yards from the ball is not enough, as a 2vl situation is easily developed and an inswinging corner can suddenly become an outswinging cross or vice-versa. In addition, the goalkeeper is paralyzed by the situation as he must wait to see what developes. As soon as the attempt at a short corner is realized, the goalkeeper must send two defenders to challenge the ball, and bring other players to the front of the goal to maintain numerical superiority.

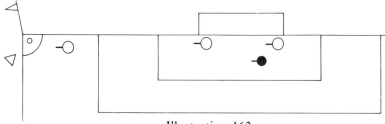

Illustration 163

2.2.2. The Direct and Indirect Free Kick (with and without a wall)

The wall is only built at the request of the goalkeeper, he must want the wall and signal for it at the moment of the foul. There should never be a wall if it is not necessary to block or otherwise divert a direct shot at goal.

As in defensive corners, defending free kicks needs extensive practice. There must be a strong understanding between the goalkeeper and the outfield player who sets up the wall, as the slightest miscommunication can result in a goal.

2.2.2.1. How Many Players in the Wall?

The number of players in the wall depends upon the angle and distance of the free kick. The following can serve as a guide.

A.   Distance of 30 yards — there is still the possibility of a specialist with a tremendous shot — if so use three players.

B.   Distance of 20 yards — use approximately 5 players.

C.   Distance of 12 to 18 yards — use approximately 8 players.

D.   Distance less than 10 yards — every player takes a position on the goal line with the goalkeeper standing in front ready to attack the ball.

NOTE: The goalkeeper can signal the number of players required by holding up the number of fingers or shouting simple, clear directions. He must not show panic.

2.2.2.2.Who Should Be in the Wall?

This should be a matter of decision for the coach, and depends upon the numbers to be used. It is important not to use all the best headers and tacklers in the wall as they are needed to win combat for the ball played over or around the wall in an indirect route to the goal. Midfielders and attackers must be quick to get back to take an active role in the wall. The two central defenders are almost always in the area of dangerous free kick situations and should be considered. Wingers, however, would be the last to join as it would be their responsibility to cover the sides of the wall for the possibility of incoming opponents or plays around the wall.

128

2.2.2.3.What is the Make Up of the Wall?

The tallest players must be at each end of the wall to block or otherwise deflect shots to the upper corners being bent around the wall. In practice, it is developed that a single player is placed to protect, in fact, over protect the near post and that the rest of the players line up to that player's inside to protect their half of the goal, and then even still every player must take a step toward the outside to further protect against the bent ball around the outside of the wall. An outfield player lines up the wall and insures its proper placement while the goalkeeper concentrates on the ball and the possibility of shots towards his half of the goal or chips over the wall, and, as well as, other multifarious situations. In all cases the goalkeeper must have clear sight of the ball and be concerned primarily with shots to the open part of the goal.

A number of free kick examples (see number in Illust. 164) are presented here for study.

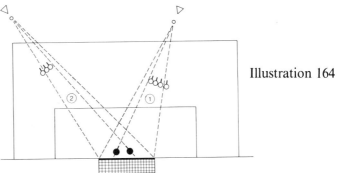

Illustration 164

Example 1. Here the goalkeeper has good sight of the ball and positions himself to the left of the middle of the goal to protect the uncovered part of the goal. The keeper must react quickly to a chip over the wall. Note the impossibility of a shot around the wall to the near post, by the over protection of that post by the full body of the first player on the wall. There is a matter of opinion regarding the line-up of the wall. Should it be parallel to the goal line or perpendicular to the possible path of the ball?

If perpendicular, as in illustration 164, it is possible for an opposing player to line-up behind the wall and still be onsides. If parallel, the opposing player would be even with the wall and in an offsides position, but the wall would cover less of the goal and an additional player may have to be utilized.

Example 2. Identical to Example 1, except the greater angle of the shot and further distance allows for one less player in the wall (see Illust. 164).

Example 3. In this instance the goalkeeper may totally discount the possibility of a shot to the near post, as it is protected by a two man wall, and the keeper can position himself for the cross. However, the goalkeeper must be aware that a left footed player may shoot an inswinger around the goalside of the wall at goal, and may be tempted to do so by the two man wall. A third player might add extra protection (see Illust. 165) and discourage a shooter.

Example 4. Here the shooting distance is very short and seven players are used . . . notice that both posts are over protected by the full body of each end player on the wall. The goalkeeper must see the ball through the legs of the wall of players and react accordingly (see Illust. 165).

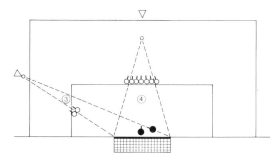

Illustration 165

FINAL NOTE: Free kicks may be taken without a whistle from the referee, providing the ball is stationary and at the approximate point of the foul. Goalkeepers must look for the opposition to take quick free kicks before the wall is set up or during the construction of the wall. The goalkeeper must never take his eyes off the ball. If the referee is forced to move back the wall, the protection provided may be reduced. After the wall is moved back by the referee he must signal for the kick to be taken, but this signal does not have to be by means of the whistle and could even be a hand gesture.

Finally, there is only one signal given by the referee to inform that the free kick is indirect, that of a hand straight up in the air. The referee will leave his hand straight up until the ball is touched or played by a second player. Indirect free kicks suddenly become dangerously direct after one rotation of the ball. Walls must be built for indirect free kicks as well.

2.2.2.4.The Open Wall

The open wall has disappeared from modern soccer and rightfully so (see Illust. 166). The danger is very high that a shot through the opening in the wall can have its direction changed by touching or deflecting off the inside part of the the body of either inside wall player. The goalkeeper reacts to the initial shot and is unable to change direction as the ball enters the goal.

Illustration 166

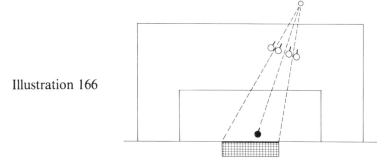

2.2.3. The Penalty Kick

2.2.3.1. Introduction

The goalkeeper must believe that the penalty kick is his finest opportunity. Almost everyone believes that the goalkeeper has no chance to save a penalty kick, and he is never really blamed when the ball hits the net, even when the shot seemed savable or should have been saved. But when the penalty kick is saved, the goalkeeper is the hero.

The chance of saving a penalty kick is certainly better than zero percent and the shooter may also be coerced into shooting wide or high. The chance of a save dramatically increases if the goalkeeper has a scouting report on the shooter, and knows everything possible about the penalty kick taker.

The penalty kick possibilities include:

A.   A precisely placed penalty kick, approximately one foot off the ground in height to either post.

B.   A power penalty kick, shot as hard as possible in the direction of the goal, even the shooter may not know exactly where it is going.

C.   The thought-out penalty kick in which the shooter does not decide the direction of the kick until the last possible moment, often after the keeper has already committed himself to either corner and then the shooter directs the ball accordingly.

What can the goalkeeper do in each above possibility?:

Example A.
1.   The goalkeeper may wait until the penalty kick is taken and dive accordingly to the corner where the kicker will be most often shooting (knowledge is power - it is best to know the kicker's choice of corner before the shot is taken).
2.   Without knowledge of the shooter, dive to the corner at which most penalty kicks are shot — right footed kicker to goalkeeper's right, left footed kicker to goalkeeper's left.

Example B. Delay diving to either corner and hope that the ball will come within the reach of the goalkeeper. A look at the direction of the runner may give the goalkeeper a clue as to the direction of the shot. The goalkeeper must depend upon reflex action to save the power penalty kick. It is often the case that the goalkeeper dives too soon and the power penalty kick hits the exact center of the back net where the goalkeeper would have been able to save.

Example C. The goalkeeper should not commit himself too soon or offer any clues as to the information that he has and the direction of his dive. The goalkeeper should not go too early and hope that the penalty kick taker is either not too sure, nor too accurate.

NOTE: The *Laws of the Game* dictate that the goalkeeper may not move his feet until after the ball is played. However, the goalkeeper may decoy the shooter or influence the shooter by way of upper body movement. Under no circumstances should the goalkeeper be guilty of ungentlemanly conduct . . . and should avoid any bizzarre or other behavior which may be deemed ungentlemanly by the referee. All concentration should be on the saving of the shot . . . this is the goalkeeper's big moment and is not the time for clowning around or anything but the utmost in seriousness.

Other clues for the goalkeeper:

A.   While placing the ball, the shooter may look briefly at the corner he is contemplating for the shot. If he stares too long into that corner, he may be trying to decoy the goalkeeper into believing the opposite.

B.   The run of the shooter (see Illust. 167). (The right footed shooter is being described, for a left footed shooter the description is reversed).

When the run is taken form the goalkeeper's right (Illust. 167), it is easiest to place the ball to the goalkeeper's left and very difficut to shoot the ball across the body. When the run is taken from the goalkeeper's left (see Illust. 168), then the shooter's best chance is to the goalkeeper's right as the shooter would need to alter his entire body position just before shooting the ball.

C.   The turning of the foot just before kicking is a good clue for the goalkeeper to study.

D.   The opening of the shooter's hips so that the ball can be placed to the opposite corner is also a good clue.

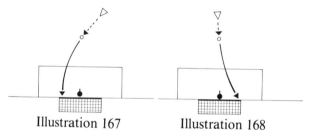

Illustration 167   Illustration 168

2.2.4. The Long Throw-In

Modern tactices dictate that a well coached team has a specialist in the taking of a long throw-in which can be placed into the penalty area, especially at the near post and flicked on across the goal to a teammate to head the ball into an often empty net. The goalkeeper must be extremely alert on all restarts, some 60% of all goals are scored from free kicks, corners, penalty-kicks and throw-ins. The goalkeeper must raise the concentration of his teammates to realize the danger from a long throw and insure that every player is tightly marked. The goalkeeper must not get caught half way . . . to the near post and allow the thrown ball to get flicked behind or past him to the far post. Being ready early will allow the goalkeeper enough time to make his play at the near post.

NOTE: There is no offside on a throw-in.

2.2.5. Referee's Ball (drop-ball)

A drop-ball in the penalty area, properly handled could result in a direct shot at goal. The goalkeeper should guarantee the organization of a wall of four players to negate the possibility of a drop-ball in the penalty area resulting in such a score. Of course, the *Laws of the Game* in college, high school and indoor soccer eliminate the possibility of a drop ball in the penalty area and F.I.F.A. is also studying this topic as a rule change.

2.2.6. The Kick-Off

Goals have been scored due to the goalkeeper's lack of concentration and poor positioning at the opening kick-off (and second half). The goalkeeper is often caught napping or inspecting the goal area. Once the ball has been played a full rotation, it may be shot directly at goal. Giving a goal on the kick-off is a sure way to shorten a goalkeeper's career.

3. Team Tactics

The goalkeeper is part of the team and must be thoroughly involved in the preparation and understanding of team tactics. Systems of play which add up to the number 10 such as 4-2-4, 4-4-2, 4-3-3 do not take into account the goalkeeper's role as sweeper for the sweeper and his distribution skills.

The time for the goalkeeper to be leaning against the post while the ball is downfield, worried only about his immediate goal area is well behind us.

The goalkeeper must be a total soccer player. He must control the entire penalty area and even beyond. If his team plays an off-side trap, then he must be ready to intercept every through ball.

The goalkeeper should not display unnecessary showmanship. . .because when it fails and the ball is in the back of the net, it causes further unrest in the team and causes a breakdown in team confidence. The keeper is the leader of the defense and total concentration is required. He can set the tone of the game with a big save early, and seriously effect the role and playing ability of his teammates through distribution which is tactically correct in relation to the score, time left, and tactical plan of his team.

In addition, the goalkeeper is tactically concerned with:

A. the playing positions of opponents;
B. tactics — home vs. away game;
C. tactics — nature of the game: league, tournament, cup or otherwise;
D. the score — ahead or trailing;
E. amount of pressure — external in relation to spectators, press, position in the standings, public image;
F. field and weather conditions — a strong wind, or sun would influence the tactical decision of short or long over the top (distribution).

Chapter Four

Conditioning

1. Jumping

Because of the height of the goal and heading as a method of scoring and preparation for scoring, the goalkeeper must have total control of the air space above the penalty area. Jumping ability (vertical jump) is an important goalkeeping attribute in the physical dimension. The recent world record for vertical jump is some 54" performed by members of the Japanese volleyball team. Yet many goalkeepers have a vertical jump as little as 20" - 24", thus handicapping their real ability to dominate the area in front of the goal. There is no substitute for good jumping ability and it cannot be faked or otherwise camouflaged. . .it needs to be developed.

The following qualities are important:
I. Jumping Power: the combination necessary to get the body high in the air.
II. Jumping Flexibility: the condition necessary to adjust the body in air, changing position to deal with various situations.
III. Jumping Reaction: the condition whereby the timing of the situation plays an important role.
IV. Jumping Endurance: the condition essential to be able to jump to the maximum in the 89th minute or overtime in a difficult game.

There are three parts to a jump as it is studied in relationship to the position of goalkeeping in soccer. These parts are separate from each other, can be dealt with separately and do not depend on each other. These movements are:
A.   the run and take-off;
B.   hanging and gliding time;
C.   landing.

Example A. The take-off can be performed off one or two legs. A goalkeeper must be able to take-off in all directions; forward, backward, sideways, left and right. Athletic ability is necessary.

Example B. There is controversy about the actuality of hanging time, but powerful jumpers seem to have both vertical and horizontal hanging time. The ball must be held higher than the jumping opponent and finally brought down as the goalkeeper prepares for his landing.

Example C. Possession of the ball greatly influences landing ability. The ball must be protected so as to not pop out of the hands, but the body must also be protected often without the use of the hands or arms. Often, the ground is the safest place for the goalkeeper. A strong vertical jump increases the realm of possibilities for the goalkeeper and flexibility will help with his landing. The ankles, knees and hips all play a part in landing properly.

Generalizations:

When training for jumping power and ability, it must be kept in mind that training for power, explosiveness, athletic ability, reaction timing, and endurance are necessary in relation to the following considerations:

1. the construction of the goalkeeper (height, weight, etc.);
2. the height of all obstacles;
3. the condition of the jumping surface;
4. weather conditions;
5. number of repetitions.

Jumping exercises without equipment:

1. Hopping with both feet, forward and backward.
2. Hopping with both feet left and right.
3. Hopping with both feet in a circle, left and right.
4. Hopping in place with feet together. . .hopping three times low, fourth time as high as possible.
5. Exercises 1, 2, 3 on one leg just left, then right.
6. Skate jumps touching toes (split jumps or squat jumps).
7. Jumping jacks.
8. Running jumps (long jump) with accent on height and distance.

Drills:

Jumping exercises with equipment:

A rope is stretched between two corner flags (see Illust. 169).

1. Repeat Exercises *1* and *2* above, first with an intermediate jump, then without.
2. Increase jump requirement through raising rope at one end (see Illust. 170). Repeat *1* and *2*.
3. Stretch two ropes between four poles as in Illustration 171:

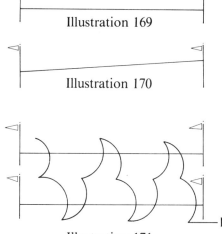

Illustration 169

Illustration 170

Illustration 171

a. with a two footed take-off jump sideways and forward with and without an intermediate jump between ropes;

b. with a one footed take-off and the other leg to the side as in hurdles, jump forward with and without an intermediate jump between ropes.

4. Exercise with hurdles (see Illust. 172):

a. forward jumping off both feet with and without an intermediate jump;

b. sideways jumping with two legs with and without an intermediate jump—jump left and right;

c. sideways with two legs over the first hurdle, back over the first hurdle and repeat now over the first and second hurdle, and then go backward over hurdle 2 and 1. Now go forward over the first three hurdles and back three etc.

5. Set up hurdles as in Illustration 173:

a. Two legged jumping over hurdle 1 with a quarter turn in the air to land facing hurdle 2. Forward jump over hurdle 2 with quarter turn to face hurdle 3 and continue.

Illustration 172   Illustration 173

b. Jump forward over the first hurdle, sideways over the second, forward over the third, sideways over the fourth etc. Up and back with and without an intermediate jump.

6. Set up hurdles as in Illustration 174.

a. Forward with two legs over the first hurdle, sideways over the second, repeat second hurdle with opposite sideways jump then forward over third, sideways over fourth, repeating etc. Up and back with and without intermediate jump.

7. Exercise with a bench or low fence (see Illust. 175).

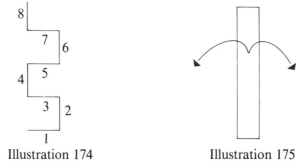

Illustration 174   Illustration 175

a.   Holding on to bench with two hands and jumping left to right, right to left.

8.   Touching the bench with one foot, first the left and then the right foot.

Exercise with the ball and other obstacles:

9.   The goalkeeper stands in the middle of the goal and dives to either post to play a ball delivered by the coach from the center. The dive must take place from a standing postion. The goalkeeper will have to alter his starting position away from the center if his jumping ablility is insufficient (see Illust. 176).

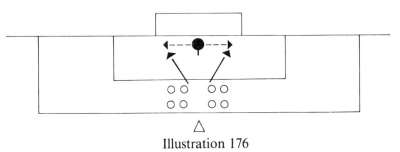

Illustration 176

Progression:
Coach plays balls:
    a.   at shoulder height;
    b.   at hip height;
    c.   along the ground;
    d.   in the upper corner;
    e.   changing haphazzardly.

10.   Obstacles are placed in the goal and all balls are served along the line of take-off . . . the ball *tells* the goalkeeper how to dive. He must respond to the visual stimulus of the served ball. Exercise 9 above is repeated except for ground balls and the goalkeeper dives over:
    a.   a player lying down;
    b.   player on his hands and knees;
    c.   player in a squat position;
    d.   a standing player bent over (Johnny on the Pony);
    e.   a hurdle or rope—be conscience of saftey factors.

11.   A rope is stretched between two poles the width of the goal. The rope starts at two feet high. The goalkeeper takes a run and jumps over the rope and directly from his landing position without any intermediate steps, dives to one of the corners to which the coach has previously indicated that the ball will be served. The ball is delivered at all heights, low, medium, and high, and the goalkeeper repeats the exercise by returning to the starting position and getting ready for his next run, jump, and service. Increase height accordingly.

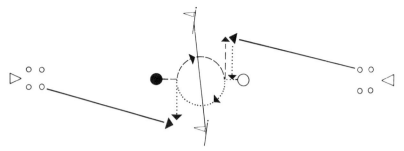

Illustration 177

12. Repeat Exercise 11 above, but now from both directions. Coach and resting goalkeeper necessary for service (see Illust. 177). From each direction.

13. A player stands in the *Johnny on the Pony* position and the goalkeeper leap-frogs over him and at the moment of landing takes off to deal with the service by the coach which can be at:

a. upper height;

b. middle height—to hip height;

c. ground level.

14. Exercise with increased demand for footwork, take-off, gliding and landing. Repeat Exercises 9, 10, 11, 12, and 13, except this time the goalkeeper must take several steps sideways before take-off and must not take-off from a stationary postion.

15. The goalkeeper hops on two feet in front of the goal in an established rhythm. The trainer tosses the ball above the crossbar. The goalkeeper catches the ball and simultaneously returns it to the coach while still in the air. The goalkeeper's hands must reach above the bar each time. He may volley the ball back to the coach if desired, but he may not be in contact with the ground at any time while he is playing the ball.

16. The goalkeeper positions himself to the back side of the goal area box, runs forward (see Illust. 178) to catch the ball above the bar and returns it

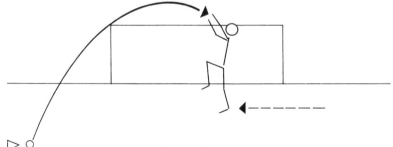

Illustration 178

to the coach before returning to the starting position. Each ball must be caught above the bar. Use the bar as a measurement.

17. Two pieces of apparatus found in many high school and college weight rooms are excellent for increasing verticle jump . . . their brand names are the *Leaper* and the *Jumper,* and their use is recommended.

18.   The *Russian Step Ladder Method* will also increase verticle jumping ability. The goalkeeper jumps off each succeeding step and absorbs the shock of landing (use soft mats or grass area) on two feet without additional movement of any kind, resisting the force to go into a deep kneebend, placing stress on the muscles used for jumping. The goalkeeper moves up and down the ladder (maximum height - six steps) for two full repetitions. After two weeks of daily activity, a five pound weight is added which the goalkeeper carrys with two hands behind his head. After two weeks the goalkeeper practices jumping up on to a bench or table without intermediate steps immediately after landing (spotters will be necessary).

2.   Muscle Strengthening Exercises

2.1.   Arm and Shoulder Girdle

A.   From a push-up position (good push-up position - body straight).
1.   Push the body up until the arms are straight, bend to the chest almost touches the ground.
2.   From the bent-lower position, explosively push-up and clap hands.
3.   From the bent-lower position with the ball between the arms, explosively push-up and land with both hands on the ball, and then to each side of the ball, repeat.

NOTE: Exercises are intensified by:
a.   increasing total number of repetitions;
b.   increasing speed or frequency of repetitions;
c.   bringing the legs higher (example: the coach may hold the feet up in the air while Exercise 3 is done on and around the ball).

B.   From a standing position with equipment.
1.   Ball boxing with two fists.
2.   Ball boxing with one fist, left and right.
3.   Ball which is tossed is boxed, two fists, one fist, left and right.
4.   All sorts of ball throwing.

a.   Replacing the regular ball with a medicine ball of 2, 4, or 10 lbs. It is better to use a rubber medicine ball because:
1.   it can stand wet weather and abrasive field conditions;
2.   it bounces;
3.   it doesn't cause injury with boxing;
4.   it can be pumped up.
b.   Increase the number of repetitions.
c.   Increase the distance.
d.   Exercise *A, B, C* - all done from sitting positions.

2.2. Stomach Muscles

A.   The goalkeeper lies down with knees tucked up and ball held in two hands. Ball is touched to the ground behind the head and then in front of the toes. Exercise should be done at top speed, then slower, again quickly, then slower.

Intensity may be increased through:
  a.   increasing the number;
  b.   increasing the speed;
  c.   use of weighted ball.

2.3. Back Muscles

A.   Lying on the stomach, grab both ankles behind, pull the back hollow and rock forward and backward (when rocking backward, put a large amount of stretch on the back muscles).

B.   Lying on the stomach, hold the ball with two hands approximately a foot and a half off the ground. Move the upper body from left to right. Change speed from quick to slow and back to quick. A difficult variation would be to bounce the ball in front of the face alternating hands with a finger tip dribble.

C.   Lying on the stomach, the ball is tossed up in the air and then tipped backward at the highest point able to be reached by the goalkeeper. The body should be raised by the strength of the back muscles, not the use of the arms.

Intensity can be increased through:
  1.   increasing the number;
  2.   increasing the frequency in a period of time;
  3.   use of the medicine ball of 2, 4 or 10 lbs.

The coach can return the ball and bring it back to the goalkeeper or as an additional fitness demand the goalkeeper must quickly get up and catch the ball before a decreasing number of bounces.

2.4. Hand and Finger Exercises

It is extremely important that the muscles of both the hands and fingers are in optimal condition for the goalkeeper to get a better grip on the ball. Top level goalkeepers do this best through the squeezing of a sponge rubber ball about the size of a baseball. Some goalkeepers have a tough rubber ring of approximately 4 inches in diameter which requires a strong grip to squeeze closed. Prior to the game many goalkeepers squeeze a tennis ball in the locker room or on the bus.

Chapter Five

Complex Training Drills

1. Objective: The improvement of dealing with crosses and the reaction to a second shot at goal.

The coach (A) serves the ball and the goalkeeper catches, distributes to the side and gets ready for a second shot that is delivered by player (B) (see Illust. 179).

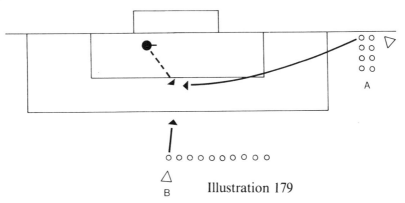

Illustration 179

NOTE: Player B should not lob the ball over the goalkeeper's head, this destroys the purpose of the exercise and discourages the goalkeeper. If the goalkeeper does not catch the ball, but is able to box it and continue its direction, player B should also shoot.

2. Objective: Improvement of reaction time, courage, mental and physical toughness.
    The coach and a player line-up at a distance of approximately 6 yards from the goal to the outside of each post each with several soccer balls. Starting from the middle the goalkeeper adjusts his position to save a direct shot at goal by the coach and then immediately runs across the goal to save a shot from the other player (see Illust. 180).

NOTE: 1.   The coach and player shoot at full strength to the short corner, then long corner and then to an unannounced corner.
    2.   The exercise should continue whether or not the goalkeeper saves and how he saved in the emergency situation is unimportant. Remember, of course, that proper technique is the best route to success.
    3.   The coach and player should give the goalkeeper a tempting amount of time to regain his position for the new situation.

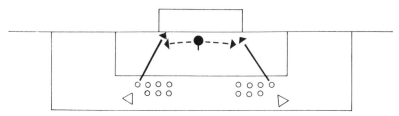

Illustration 180

3. Objective: Quick movement in the goal in dealing with high and low shots (see Illust. 181).

A. The coach plays a high ball to the right of the goalkeeper. The keeper saves and rolls the ball back to the coach who in the meantime has shot a second ball low to the other corner which the keeper moves quickly to save.

B. Change sides — high and low.

NOTE: The goalkeeper must try not to fail. . .the coach must demand effort and quickness in the goal.

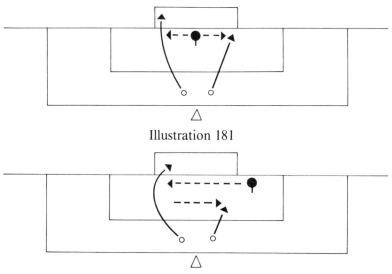

Illustration 181

Illustration 182

4. Objective: The improvement of quick movement in the goal and agility (violent change of direction - see Illust. 182).

A. The goalkeeper stands to the side of the goal and runs across the goal to catch a ball out of the air served high by the coach; then turns around quickly to save a low ball tossed into the corner. The coach serves from about the penalty spot.

B. Repeat *A*, but change sides.

5.   Objective: Intensive training for the maintenance of reaction time and the improvement of overall conditioning.

A.   From the center of the field players dribble towards the goal. Shots are taken from the top of the penalty area. Goalkeeper saves first shot and immediately gets ready for the second. Third player hunts rebounds or can be a third shooting player.

B.   From the center line again, balls are played forward to a target player who squares the ball off and the passing player shoots first time. Goalkeeper saves and gets up quickly for the second and third shots (see Illust. 184). As in *A* above, the tempo is kept fast.

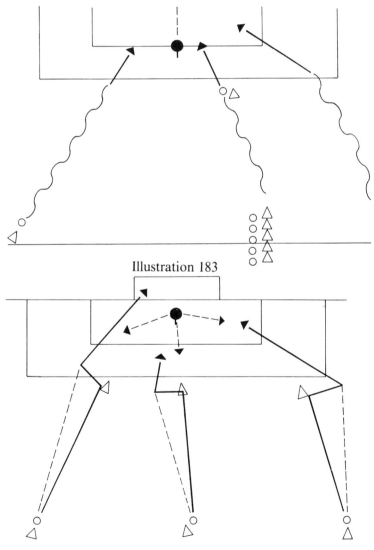

Illustration 183

Illustration 184

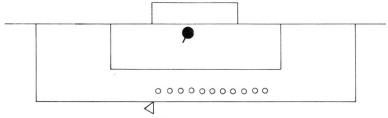

Illustration 185

C. See Illustration 185. The coach plays the first ball into a decided corner. The goalkeeper knows the corner and the pressure is to catch the ball. The second ball is shot into the opposite corner, and the demand is the same as the goalkeeper must get up quickly and save at the opposite corner.

Illustration 186

D. Same as C above, but the balls are placed in different order and line as in the two examples in Illustration 186.

6. Objective: Sharpening and maintaining reflexes.

A. Coach shoots the balls quickly at full strength to the goalkeeper's body or just to the side of the goalkeeper with rapid repetition. The keeper saves with his feet, legs, body, arms, hands, whatever. Technical saving is not important, but the defending is what counts (see Illust. 187). Exercise can also be done with a screening player interferring with the goalkeeper's vision.

B. Same as 6 above, but with a drop-kick.

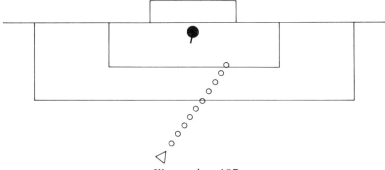

Illustration 187

7. Objective: Improvement of quick movement in front of the goal.

A. Player A serves a low shot along the ground to the post; the goalkeeper with footwork dives to save the ball and quickly returns the ball to shooter A while at the same time a ball is shot by player B low to the opposite post, the keeper continues to save at both posts (see Illust. 188).

B. On the signal from the coach, the goalkeeper starts at the center, runs over to touch the goalpost then goes full length across the goal to save a low ball delivered by the coach to the opposite post. The goalkeeper then returns the ball to the coach, resumes his position in the middle of the goal and waits for the next signal (see Illust. 189).

144

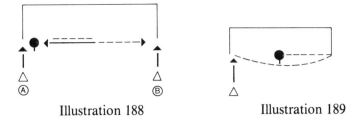

Illustration 188   Illustration 189

C.   Same as *B* above, but the starting position changes to include starting from a sitting position, lying on the stomach, lying on the back, push-up position etc.

D.   Same as *B* above, but the ball is served at varying heights. This way the goalkeeper must fall, dive, fly and catch, tip or box the ball.

E.   Same as *D* above, but change starting positions as in *C* above.

NOTE: Training must be done to both sides - left and right.

F.   The coach serves a ball low to one of two sides. The goalkeeper saves accordingly and plays back to the coach. The goalkeeper immediately gets up, runs to touch the other post and save a ball thrown high in the air by the coach before it bounces a second time (see Illust. 190).

Variation: The goalkeeper standing at one post, serves a ball as high and straight in the air as possible, then runs across the goal to save a low ball thrown by the coach. The goalkeeper returns the saved ball to the coach and immediately gets up to catch the first ball which he threw high before it bounces a second time.

G.   Same as *F,* but change starting sides.

H.   See Illustration 191:

a.   a ball is played into the corner, then

b.   a ball is served with an arch which the keeper must come out and get before it bounces, then

c.   a lob is put over the goalkeeper's head and he must run back quickly to either tip the ball, box or catch it.

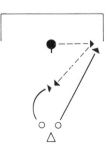

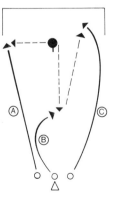

Illustration 190   Illustration 191

I.   Same as *H* above, but change starting sides.

J.   See illustration 192:

a.   player A plays the ball high near the far post;

b.   player B shoots a straight shot along the ground down the center of the goal. The goalkeeper runs diagonally forward to save the low shot;

c.   player C plays a high ball to the far post which the goalkeeper must deal with. The keeper then returns to the middle to start over.

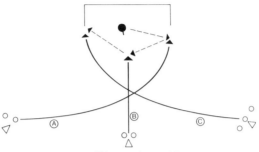

Illustration 192

K.   Repeat J above, but start in the opposite direction.

L.   See illustration 193:

a.   ball A is shot into the corner of the goal;

b.   ball B is tossed with an arch to get the goalkeeper out of the goal. He should attempt to catch the ball before it bounces;

c.   ball C is lobbed or bent around the keeper;

d.   ball D is played to the other corner.

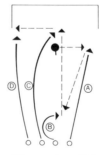

Illustration 193

NOTE: The goalkeeper should work hard in these intensive training exercises for a period of 40 seconds of non-stop activity. He should then rest for 40 seconds while the back-up goalkeeper is put through the same routine. Each exercise must be worked to both the right and left.

If each goalkeeper participates in ten exercises to the right and ten to the left for a 40 second period, given a ten to twenty second period in between exercises to set up each new drill, retrieve balls, change keepers etc., the total time consumed should amount to approximately 40 minutes. A terrific training session for both goalkeepers. Many goalkeepers who believe they are fit have difficulty with 6 to 10 stints. Twenty is the objective, ten to each side.

146

Chapter Six

LAWS OF THE GAME THAT APPLY TO THE GOALKEEPER
— The goalkeeper's uniform (jersey) must be a different color than all the other players (teammates and opposition), as well as that of the referee.
— The constantly changing 4 step rule and the attempt to tighten up the goalkeeper's ability to waste time now prohibits the goalkeeper from playing the ball with his hands after he has been in possession of the ball unless it has been played by another player. As predicted, another rule change has come to be, forcing the goalkeeper to play the ball out of the penalty area before he can receive it back to be played by hand.
— Outside of the penalty area, the goalkeeper has no special privileges, the same rules that apply to an outfield player, apply to the goalkeeper.
— Goal-kicks and free kicks in favor of the goalkeeper's team which occur in his own goal area may be taken from any place within the goal area providing they are taken on the proper side of an imaginary line dividing the center of the goal area to the goal line.
It is not a goal until the entire ball crosses the goal line.
— A goal cannot be scored directly from a kick-off, throw-in, or indirect free kick. The ball must be touched by a second player after it has traveled the distance of its own circumference.
— There is no off-side on a goal-kick, corner kick, throw-in, and drop ball . . . when the ball is being played initially at that instance.
— On penalty kicks, the ball may be played a second time by the shooter if it has been touched by the goalkeeper, but not if it rebounds to the shooter off the post or crossbar having not been touched by the goalkeeper.
— The goalkeeper may not move his feet until the ball has been played in penalty kick situations. Referees are beginning to seriously tighten up on these violations.
— If the goalkeeper is guilty of time wasting, he may be officially cautioned by the referee (yellow card). If such time wasting occurs while the ball is in play (lengthy lying on the ball - failure to distribute or otherwise play the ball) an indirect free kick may be awarded to the opposition from the point of infraction.
— Any serious foul (direct foul) committed by the goalkeeper within the penalty area will result in a penalty kick awarded to the opposition. The following are the direct fouls which apply: pushing, holding, charging from behind, charging in a violent or dangerous manner, striking, kicking, tripping, jumping at.
— The less serious (indirect) fouls will result in an indirect free kick: obstruction, dangerous play, legal charge not in playing distance of the ball (shoulder to shoulder).
— The goalkeeper may be charged legally (shoulder to shoulder - in playing distance of the ball), when he has passed outside of the goal area, is obstructing (actually shielding) the ball from an opponent or when he is in fact holding the ball. Most referees consider all charging of the goalkeeper to be in violation of the law, but it is important to know that the goalkeeper may be legally charged in the above circumstances.

Chapter Seven

PRACTICAL GOALKEEPING TIPS
— Always be concerned with preparation.
— Be aware of the special qualities of the opposition - how they take free kicks, corners, penalty kicks, any special shooting traits.
— Inspect your equipment bag before leaving for the game - check your game shoes, gloves and all other articles as they are packed.
— Concentration level must always be high . . . it is the only way to play well at goalkeeper and avoid unnecesary injuries.
— Choose your own warm-up and standardize it for you. The warm-up should always be the same and for your benefit regardless of the nature of the game . . . from exhibition game to championship game.
— Be ready at the first whistle - the safest place for the ball is in your hands. Do not react to feints and ploys by the opponents - concentrate solely on the ball and your job.
— The decision of the referee is binding - do not lose your concentration by unnecessary over-reaction to an official decision.
— Go to meet the ball whenever and where ever possible, do not underestimate the oppponent's ability to beat you to the ball as they can come from all sides and even from behind you.
— Once you decide to leave the goal, go through with it, do not hesitate and never get caught half-way or retreating.
— Stay steady rather than looking to be spectacular, an over concern with style or flamboyancy will work against the goalkeeper in the long run. The important thing is the goals against.
— Organize the defense with short and precise instructions and information. Do not become a cheerleader or blabber mouth.
— The responsibility to play with injury is yours . . . only you know when the injury hampers your ability to play in either the physical, technical or psychological dimension. There are important decisions to be made in this regard and you must provide the coach or medical personnel with proper guidance . . . understand that playing in pain is part of goalkeeping.
— Take all goal kicks . . . it is part of your job . . . do not force your team to play further short-handed by having a teammate take the goal kick.
— Always realize that it is impossible to learn everything about goalkeeping and that the position of goalkeeper requires a life-time of study. Look for new ideas and training tips. Study the goalkeepers in the world of international soccer.

For further information, write Joe Machnik, c/o No. 1 Goalkeeper's Camp, P.O. Box 107, Branford, CT 06405 — or call 1-800-MACHNIK.

Joseph A. Machnik

Frans Hoek